YORK NOTES

Jude the Obscure

Thomas Hardy

Note by Julian Cowley

Longman   York Press

Julian Cowley is hereby identified as author of this work in accordance with Section 77 of the Copyright, Designs and Patents Act 1988

YORK PRESS
322 Old Brompton Road, London SW5 9JH

PEARSON EDUCATION LIMITED
Edinburgh Gate, Harlow,
Essex CM20 2JE, United Kingdom
Associated companies, branches and representatives throughout the world

First published 2001

ISBN 0–582–43163–8

Designed by Vicki Pacey
Phototypeset by Gem Graphics, Trenance, Mawgan Porth, Cornwall
Colour reproduction and film output by Spectrum Colour
Produced by Addison Wesley Longman China Limited, Hong Kong

CONTENTS

PART ONE

INTRODUCTION   How to Study a Novel   5
                 Reading *Jude the Obscure*   6

PART TWO

SUMMARIES & COMMENTARIES
                 A Note on the Text   7
                 Synopsis   7
                 Detailed Summaries   8
                   Part First: At Marygreen   8
                   Part Second: At Christminster   20
                   Part Third: At Melchester   29
                   Part Fourth: At Shaston   38
                   Part Fifth: At Aldbrickham and Elsewhere   48
                   Part Sixth: At Christminster Again   56

PART THREE

CRITICAL APPROACHES
                 Characterisation   69
                   Jude Fawley   69
                   Richard Phillotson   72
                   Arabella Donn   73
                   Sue Bridehead   74
                   Little Father Time   77
                   Minor Characters   78
                 Themes   79
                   Modern Restlessness   79
                   Individual Lives & Historical Periods   81
                   Ideal Forms & Material Reality   82
                   Relativism   83
                 Language & Style   83

Narrative Structure & Technique 85
   Structure 85
   Narration 85
   Patterning 86
   Irony 87
   Animal Imagery 87
   Satire 88
   Environment 89

PART FOUR

TEXTUAL ANALYSIS
   Text 1: (from Part Second, Chapter 2) 90
   Text 2: (from Part Third, Chapter 1) 94
   Text 3: (from Part Sixth, Chapter 2) 97

PART FIVE

BACKGROUND
   Hardy's Life & Work 102
     His Writings 103
   Historical Background 104
     Thomas Malthus 104
     The Declining Importance of Agriculture 105
     Education 105
     Loss of Religious Faith 106
     Railways 107
   Literary Background 108
     Shelley 108
     The Nineteenth-Century Novel 109

PART SIX

CRITICAL HISTORY & BROADER PERSPECTIVES
   Reception & Early Critical Reviews 111
   Critical Responses 111
   Contemporary Approaches 114
     Feminist 114
     Structuralist 116
     Psychological 117

Chronology 119
Literary Terms 122
Author of this Note 123

Part one

Introduction

How to study a novel

Studying a novel on your own requires self-discipline and a carefully thought-out work plan in order to be effective.

- You will need to read the novel more than once. Start by reading it quickly for pleasure, then read it slowly and thoroughly.
- On your second reading make detailed notes on the plot, characters and themes of the novel. Further readings will generate new ideas and help you to memorise the details of the story.
- Some of the characters will develop as the plot unfolds. How do your responses towards them change during the course of the novel?
- Think about how the novel is narrated. From whose point of view are events described?
- A novel may or may not present events chronologically: the time-scheme may be a key to its structure and organisation.
- What part do the settings play in the novel?
- Are words, images or incidents repeated so as to give the work a pattern? Do such patterns help you to understand the novel's themes?
- Identify what styles of language are used in the novel.
- What is the effect of the novel's ending? Is the action completed and closed, or left incomplete and open?
- Does the novel present a moral and just world?
- Cite exact sources for all quotations, whether from the text itself or from critical commentaries. Wherever possible find your own examples from the novel to back up your opinions.
- Always express your ideas in your own words.

This York Note offers an introduction to *Jude the Obscure* and cannot substitute for close reading of the text and the study of secondary sources.

Jude the Obscure may be read not as a single novel but a whole range of potential novels. Your point of view as a reader will determine which one you read. Is it the ironic culmination of the great tradition of Victorian fiction? Or is it a breakthrough into new ways of writing, heralding the imminent arrival of the twentieth century? Is it an odd departure from Thomas Hardy's memorable series of Wessex novels? Or is it the apt conclusion of that sequence? Does it embody a tragic vision of life? Or is it a farce comprising ludicrous situations and grotesque distortions? Does it contemplate the modern world with gloomy resignation? Or is it an incisive satire addressing social injustice and oppression? Is it a novel about Jude Fawley? Or a novel about Sue Bridehead? Or is Arabella Donn the novel's real heroine?

Critical discussion has elicited strikingly divergent responses. This may suggest a flaw in Thomas Hardy's writing. Or it may confirm the novelist's achievement in producing a work that embodies the contradictions and unresolvable tensions of modern living. Certainly, *Jude the Obscure* is an unsettling and challenging novel, a book that lodges in the memory, however you may choose to read it.

PART TWO

SUMMARIES & COMMENTARIES

Jude the Obscure *initially appeared in serial form in* Harper's New Monthly Magazine *between December 1894 and November 1895. The Penguin edition used for this* Note *reprints the first edition in book form, published in London by Osgood, McIlvaine in 1895, yet postdated 1896. Macmillan published the novel as part of a Uniform edition of Thomas Hardy's work in 1903.*

The standard edition of Thomas Hardy's novels is the Wessex Edition, issued by Macmillan, in 24 volumes, between 1912 and 1931. Most of these volumes were prepared for publication by the author himself. A New Wessex Edition appeared in 1974–5, with an introduction to Jude the Obscure *written by the Marxist critic, Terry Eagleton.*

SYNOPSIS

Following the death of his parents, Jude Fawley is raised by his great-aunt Drusilla in the village of Marygreen. Aged eleven, Jude watches his schoolmaster, Richard Phillotson, depart for Christminster, driven by his aspiration to enter the city's university. Jude is fired by a similar ambition, and pursues his own studies while doing mundane work for his aunt.

Five years later, Jude becomes an apprentice stonemason in Alfredston. A few years after that he meets and marries Arabella Donn. Three years on, Arabella leaves Jude, who then goes to Christminster, where he meets his cousin, Sue Bridehead. Jude falls in love with Sue, but after seeing her courted by Phillotson he returns to Marygreen.

Sue learns that Jude is married, and that precipitates her marriage to Phillotson. Before long she leaves her husband and joins Jude at Aldbrickham, where they live contentedly and have two children. Both couples are formally divorced. Phillotson's fortunes decline steeply.

After abandoning Jude and travelling to Australia with her parents, Arabella gave birth to his son. This child, known as Little Father Time,

joins Jude and Sue, who look after him. The couple take their family to
Christminster, where Little Father Time kills the other children and
commits suicide. Sue returns to Phillotson and remarries. Arabella,
hearing of this development, seeks out Jude and contrives to remarry him.
Jude grows increasingly ill. He visits Sue and asks her to run away with
him. At last, while university festivities occur around his lodgings, Jude
dies, alone.

PART FIRST: AT MARYGREEN

CHAPTER 1   Jude Fawley watches Richard Phillotson depart for
             Christminster

Richard Phillotson, a schoolmaster, leaves the village of Marygreen and
moves to Christminster, in the hope that he may eventually study at the
city's university, and be ordained as a clergyman. Jude Fawley, an eleven-
year-old orphan who has attended the teacher's evening classes, sadly
watches him depart. Phillotson gives Jude a book as a farewell present.

> Thomas Hardy based Marygreen on Fawley, a Berkshire village
> from which Jude takes his surname. Christminster is based on
> Oxford.
>
> The novel shows this part of England in a state of transition, and
> the processes of change are evident even in secluded Marygreen,
> where trees have been felled, old houses demolished, and the
> ancient church replaced by a new building. It is a crucial part of
> Jude's story that he lives during such a transitional phase of history
> (see Themes, on Individual Lives & Historical Periods).
>
> The opening chapter highlights the age difference between Jude,
> aged eleven, and Phillotson, in his early thirties. This difference
> assumes significance later, when they become rivals for the love of
> Sue Bridehead. Young Jude respects the older man's learning and is
> fired with desire to emulate him. As the narrative unfolds, the lives
> of these characters become closely interlinked.
>
> Phillotson is moving to temporary lodgings. Reliance upon such
> impermanent accommodation is a feature of this novel, where long-

established and relatively stable ways of life within rural communities are seen to be disrupted by personal ambition and increased mobility (see Themes, on Modern Restlessness).

ESDRAS from the biblical Apocrypha, the First Book of Edras 4:26, 27 and 32

certain historic disciples a reference to the response to Christ's crucifixion recorded in Luke 23:48–9

German-Gothic design the Gothic Revival style, popular in Victorian England

CHAPTER 2   **Aunt Drusilla advises Jude never to marry. He is dismissed from his job as a bird-scarer, because he is too sympathetic towards rooks. He conceives the idea of going to Christminster**

Jude has lived, since the death of his parents, with his great-aunt Drusilla, Marygreen's baker. Jude overhears her talking with other villagers of Phillotson's prospects. Jude is said to be 'crazy for books', just like his cousin Sue (p. 13). Aunt Drusilla admonishes him not to marry, as the Fawleys have experienced unhappiness in marriage.

Jude works as a bird-scarer for a farmer named Troutham. Recalling Phillotson's injunction to be kind to birds and animals, he allows rooks to feed. Troutham beats Jude before dismissing him from the job. Jude conceives the idea of going to Christminster.

Drusilla speaks a distinctive Wessex **dialect**. Her speech includes vocabulary and grammatical idiosyncrasies peculiar to the region where she has spent her entire life. Thomas Hardy uses this dialect to show the narrow geographical limits of this woman's experience. As his characters gain access to the modern world, especially through education, they shed their local variant English and start to speak more standardised English (see Language & Style).

Drusilla's description of Jude as a 'poor useless boy' (p. 13) who would be better off dead fuels the boy's awakening determination to make something of his life. Jude senses 'A magic thread of fellow-feeling' that connects the unwanted rooks' existence to his own (p. 15).

tassets of mail overlapping plates on a suit of armour
as Job said reference to Job 30:1

CHAPTER 3   Jude first glimpses the distant city of Christminster,
and hears of its reputation for learning

Jude walks towards Christminster. After a few miles, he meets some
workmen and discusses the location of the city with them. At evening he
climbs a ladder they have left and as the mist disperses he sees the distant
city, which takes on a mystical significance.

On another evening he wanders out of Marygreen in order to see
the distant lights again. He encounters a carter who tells him of
Christminster's reputation for sophisticated learning. Jude feels intensely
drawn to the place and its erudition.

> The mist shrouding the distant city serves as a symbol of Jude's
> indistinct perception and vague understanding of what awaits him
> in Christminster. It foreshadows the thick fog which cloaks the city
> in the closing chapters, symbolising the mental confusion into
> which Jude has been thrown at that point.

> Jude, with a child's limited and superstitious grasp of Christian
> belief, prays for the mist to rise. It eventually does so, as if in good
> omen. At the end of the novel, Jude has abandoned Christian faith
> and entertains no thought that prayer might ameliorate the
> conditions in which his life is led.

heavenly Jerusalem Revelation 21:2; St John's vision of a holy city
descending from heaven
Herne the Hunter legendary wild hunter
Apollyon lying in wait for Christian John Bunyan (1628–88), in *The Pilgrim's
Progress* (1678, 1684) describes Christian's meeting with the monstrous
Apollyon in the Valley of Humiliation
the bewitched ship taken from 'The Story of the Ghost Ship' by the German
writer Wilhelm Haüff (1802–27)
the Apocalyptic writer St John, author of Revelation
Nebuchadnezzar's furnace in Daniel 3:24–5, God protects Shadrach,
Meshach, and Abednego who are consigned to a furnace by the Babylonian
king, Nebuchadnezzar, for refusing to worship an idol
the city of light in Matthew 5:14
tree of knowledge in Genesis 2:17

CHAPTER 4   **Jude is duped by the fraudulent doctor Vilbert. Phillotson sends Jude books of grammar and he starts to tackle Greek and Latin**

Jude walks towards his home, in company with Vilbert, 'an itinerant quack-doctor' (p. 26). They talk of Christminster, and Jude expresses his desire to learn Greek and Latin. Vilbert promises to give Jude books of grammar for those languages, if he secures customers for his medicines. A fortnight later, Jude gives Vilbert a list of potential purchasers, but the fraudulent physician has no books.

Phillotson sends for his piano which is stored at Aunt Drusilla's house. Jude writes a note to the schoolmaster, asking if he can send him grammar books. Two books arrive. Jude is initially overwhelmed by the work required to learn another language.

Jude is now twelve. He again wishes he had not been born. This tendency to despair is offset by excitement at the prospect of entering the world of scholarship. His son, Little Father Time, will display deeper pessimism, without the balancing effects of inquisitiveness and aspiration.

During the nineteenth century the practice of medicine became increasingly professionalised. Vilbert sells folk remedies, of the kind which had treated health problems in rural communities for centuries, but were becoming outmoded. Vilbert is not an authentic healer using ancient methods, nor a modern scientific practitioner, but a fraudulent dealer in pills and potions, exploiting the gullibility of the rural poor, with their limited education.

Mount Sinai of sacred importance to Christians, Jews and Muslims
Grimm's Law a law of historical change establishing relationships between different languages, formulated by Jakob Grimm (1785–1863)
Israel in Egypt Exodus 1:13–14

CHAPTER 5   **Jude devotes himself to learning Greek and Latin, but
determines to use them to Christian ends. He becomes
an apprentice stonemason, a trade that will enable him
to move to Christminster**

Jude's perception of the effort involved in acquiring another language
enhances his respect for Christminster's scholarly inhabitants. He delivers
bread for his aunt, studying rudimentary Latin as he allows the horse to
steer the cart. A policeman cautions him for driving with inadequate care.

Alarmed at his own immersion in pagan literature he shifts to the
New Testament in Greek, and starts to visit local churches, deciphering
Latin inscriptions. In order to learn a trade that will make viable a move
to Christminster, he becomes apprenticed to a stonecutter in Alfredston.
Later, he works for an ecclesiastical architect, helping to restore local
churches.

This chapter summarises Jude's life between the ages of sixteen and
nineteen.

Jude's simple Christian faith prompts him to curb his youthful
desire for knowledge as an end in itself, and he envisages
scholarship enabling him to become a clergyman. Throughout the
novel, the difficulty of sustaining Christian faith is evident (see
Historical Background, on Loss of Religious Faith), especially
given the attractions of other ways of viewing the world, such as the
pagan philosophies of ancient Greece (see Themes, on Relativism).

In the course of the narrative, Jude moves from Christian belief
to disbelief, while Sue Bridehead follows an opposite course
from paganism to Christianity. In this chapter, Sue is mentioned
for the second time. It is a passing reference, but Thomas Hardy
is preparing us for the prominence she later assumes in Jude's
life.

Caesar Julius Caesar, Roman soldier, politician and writer (100–44BC)
Virgil Latin poet (70–19BC)
Horace Latin poet (65–8BC)
Delphine editions a series of annotated editions of Latin works, prepared in
seventeenth-century France for the education of the Dauphin

Dido in Virgil's *Aeneid*, Book IV, Dido, Queen of Carthage, commits suicide when abandoned by Aeneas

laying the sponge part of the breadmaking process

Carmen Saeculare poem by Horace

shiny goddess moon

'Phoebe silvarumque potens Diana' (Latin) Phoebus and Diana, ruler of the woods

Homer Greek poet (eighth century BC)

Ionic ancient Greek dialect

Griesbach's text Johann Griesbach (1745–1812) produced an edition of the New Testament in Greek

the Fathers *The Oxford Library of Fathers of the Holy Catholic Church, anterior to the Division of the East and West* (1838–57), in 48 volumes

CHAPTER 6   **Jude meets Arabella Donn**

Jude, now nineteen years old, returns for the weekend from Alfredston to Marygreen. He looks forward to a time when he can make his living in Christminster. He considers his progress in learning Latin and Greek, and envisages admission to the university as a student. One day, perhaps, he will become a bishop. As these elevated thoughts run through his mind he is disturbed by the taunts of a group of young women, washing pig's entrails on the other side of a hedge. He talks to one of them, Arabella Donn, and is attracted by her sensuality. They arrange to meet on the following day.

Jude's intellectual and spiritual aspirations are contrasted with the unalloyed physicality of the young women and their work. But he has reached a stage in his life when sexual attraction exercises a powerful influence over his behaviour. Thomas Hardy shows Jude's life to be shaped by social forces over which he has no control, but also by physical drives of which he is only partially aware.

Arabella, on the other hand, is portrayed as a calculating seductress. She knowingly forms dimples which add to her attractiveness. Jude blushes, a physical response over which he has no conscious control. Physical desire now vies with intellectual and spiritual aspiration within his character. Jude recognises that Arabella is the antithesis of his refined hopes and goals, but this perception is soon obscured by his aroused sexuality.

Hesiod Greek epic poet (eighth century BC)

Thucydides Greek historian (fifth century BC)

Euclid Greek mathematician (fourth century BC)

Livy Roman historian (59BC–AD17)

Tacitus Roman historian (c.55–117)

Herodotus Greek historian (c.480–c.380BC)

Aeschylus Greek tragic dramatist (525–456BC)

Sophocles Greek tragic dramatist (c.496–406BC)

Aristophanes Greek comic dramatist (c.448–c.380BC)

Euripides Greek tragic dramatist (480–406BC)

Plato Greek philosopher (c.427–348BC)

Aristotle Greek philosopher (384–322BC)

Lucretius Roman poet (c.99–55BC)

Epictetus Roman philosopher (c.60–140)

Seneca Roman philosopher and tragic dramatist (c.4BC–AD65)

Antoninus Roman emperor and philosopher (121–180)

Bede English monk and ecclesiastical historian (673–735)

Alma Mater (Latin, literally 'caring mother') applied by former students to the educational institution from which they graduated

the characteristic part of a barrow-pig the penis of a castrated boar

chitterlings pig's small intestine, later minced and cooked

in posse (Latin) possible but not actual

CHAPTER 7   Jude and Arabella walk to Alfredston

On Sunday afternoon, instead of reading his Greek New Testament as he had planned, Jude meets Arabella. They walk and talk in the vicinity of her house. Reaching the Brown House barn they see smoke rising from a building in the distance. At Arabella's insistence, they walk three miles to the site of the fire.

They stop for tea at an inn in Alfredston. Onlookers remark that Jude seems to be courting a girl who is his social inferior. After drinking beer, Jude kisses Arabella as they walk home.

> Thomas Hardy uses **metaphor** to build a sense that Jude is not in control of his actions, that other forces are at work. The attraction drawing him to Arabella, against his better judgement, is said to be 'a compelling arm of extraordinary muscular power' (p. 44).

Elaborating his metaphor, Hardy compares this arm to that of a violent schoolmaster, using bullying force upon a schoolboy. The intensely physical image produced by this simile makes a striking contrast to the apparently beneficial influence that Richard Phillotson has had upon his pupil Jude.

Jude the Obscure contains many allusions to the Bible. This is ironic given that the authority of the Bible was being called into question by influential figures amongst Thomas Hardy's contemporaries (see Historical Background, on Loss of Religious Faith). This novel offers no consoling picture of a benign God, but it does suggest the continuing practical relevance of biblical texts to the lives of modern men and women.

Reference to the biblical tale of Samson and Delilah is relevant to this novel in which a man appears to be betrayed and fatally weakened by the actions of two women. Of course, such a reading might be countered with another which proposes that Jude's failure is a consequence of his own flawed character, rather than the influence of Arabella or Sue. Another reading might argue convincingly that all three are helpless victims of circumstances that lie beyond their control.

At the inn, Arabella displays her knowledge of beer. Later on she will become a publican's wife, drawing upon her extensive worldly education in the ways of public houses. Jude, on the other hand, comes to recognise excessive drinking as a weakness in his character. He drinks out of desperation and lacks Arabella's understanding of alcohol. This will enable her repeatedly to manipulate him to her own ends, notably when she persuades Jude to marry her for a second time.

H ΚΑΙΝΗ ΔΙΑΘΗΚΗ (Greek) the New Testament

Samson and Delilah Judges 16; Delilah, acting for the Philistines, discovers that the key to Samson's strength resides in his uncut hair

CHAPTER 8   **Jude returns to Marygreen and visits Arabella**

At the end of the working week, Jude returns to Marygreen, going out of his way in order to see Arabella as soon as possible. He helps her catch some small pigs which have escaped from their sty. One evades capture, and heads towards the farm from which it has recently been purchased. Arabella is confident the pig will be returned. She refuses to kiss Jude and, when they reach her home, says farewell in an aloof manner.

On Sunday morning, Arabella hears from a neighbour that Jude intends to move to Christminster. She arranges with her mother to have their house to herself that evening, and after walking with Jude in the afternoon they return there. She shows him a bantam's egg she is incubating in her bosom, and teasingly explains that he is consequently not allowed to touch her. He seizes the egg, then pursues her upstairs.

A **simile** compares Jude to 'a pet lamb' (p. 53). Arabella on the other hand is said to make a 'tigerish indrawing of breath' (p. 54). Animal **imagery** is used regularly throughout the novel to cast light upon aspects of character and behaviour.

In this instance, we may recognise that the piglet, who makes a break for freedom but will be returned inevitably to the Donn family, suggests parallels with the course of Jude's life. No direct comparison is made between Jude and the piglet, but similes elsewhere that overtly compare him and other characters to animals invite us to make the connection here.

CHAPTER 9   Jude announces his intention to leave the area.
Arabella responds by announcing that she is pregnant.
After their marriage, she reveals that she is not, after all, expecting a child

Jude and Arabella see one another constantly during the ensuing two months. One day, he tells her he is going away, and believes that parting will be best for both of them. She tells him she is pregnant, and Jude agrees to marry her. The marriage takes place, and they live in a cottage between Marygreen and the Brown House. Jude walks to Alfredston daily. Arabella keeps a pig and grows vegetables.

Arabella discloses to her friend Anny that she is not in fact pregnant. Eventually, reluctantly, she reveals this to Jude. He is appalled that he has been hurried into marriage under false pretences. She responds by saying, 'What's done can't be undone' (p. 61).

Jude's ideals continually run into obstacles posed by physical circumstances. More generally, Thomas Hardy shows ideal conceptions of reality falling foul of material conditions (see Themes, on Ideal Forms & Material Reality). The notion that marital vows can ensure a harmonious relationship between husband and wife is repeatedly subjected to **satirical** treatment.

The narrator reports that 'the two swore that at every other time of their lives they would assuredly believe, feel, and desire precisely as they had believed, felt, and desired during the few preceding weeks' (pp. 57–8). The tone is ironic, mocking the assumption that marriage can sustain the initial attraction felt between lovers. In Part First, Chapter 11, Jude feels that his life, and Arabella's, have been ruined by 'the fundamental error of their matrimonial union: that of having based a permanent contract on a temporary feeling which had no necessary connection with affinities that alone render a life-long companionship tolerable' (p. 69).

CHAPTER 10 **Jude slaughters a pig. On another day, not long afterwards, he overhears Arabella's friends gossiping about her ruse to ensnare Jude. He confronts her with this accusation**

One morning, heavy snow delays the arrival of a man named Challow, who has been engaged to slaughter Jude and Arabella's pig. Jude has to kill the animal himself. Arabella insists the death must be slow in order to increase the value of the meat, but Jude cannot bear such cruelty and hastens the pig's death. Arabella silences the dying creature by slitting its windpipe. She is angered when Jude accidentally kicks over the bucket of blood she planned to use to make black pudding. Challow arrives after the killing has been completed. Jude goes to work in Alfredston.

One day, passing the spot where he first met Arabella, Jude chances to hear her friends talking about the ruse she had used to ensnare him in marriage. Uncertain of the details, Jude is nonetheless distressed. After supper with his aunt, he arrives home late and confronts Arabella, who is melting down pig fat, with the charge that she deliberately sought to become pregnant in order to trap him. He now regards their marriage as a 'life-long penalty' (p. 67).

In the opening chapter, Phillotson instructs Jude to be kind to animals and birds. Jude finds the prospect of killing a pig abhorrent. Arabella calls him a 'tender-hearted fool' (p. 64), and takes control of the situation, demonstrating once again her superiority in terms of practical knowledge. Jude thanks God when he sees the pig is dead. Arabella replies: 'What's God got to do with such a messy job as a pig-killing, I should like to know!' (p. 65). She has no sense of the involvement of a transcendent God in the physical events of the material world.

In Part First, Chapter 8 animal **imagery** serves as a prompt for us to recognise parallels between the fate of a piglet and the course of Jude's life. Here the slaughtered pig is said to look at Arabella as it dies 'with the eloquently keen reproach of a creature recognizing at last the treachery of those who seemed his only friends' (p. 64). Jude repeatedly appears the victim of treachery on the part of those he considers friends, including Arabella, who has already trapped him into marriage by feigning pregnancy.

CHAPTER 11   Arabella accuses Jude of being an abusive husband, and says that such behaviour is characteristic of his family. Aunt Drusilla confirms that Jude's father and aunt had unhappy marriages. Arabella leaves Jude, intending to emigrate to Australia. Jude's earlier ambitions revive

Next morning, Arabella, resentful of Jude's accusation, flings some of his books on to the floor. He is furious, and restrains her. Once released, she walks along the road, with hair dishevelled and buttons of her gown undone. Passers-by are alarmed at her appearance. She has pig fat on her hands and proclaims that Jude not only makes her work on Sunday, but mistreats her physically. Jude's initial anger is displaced by awareness that their relationship has run its course. Arabella suggests that Jude's father and his father's sister similarly practised abuse within marriage.

Jude visits aunt Drusilla and questions her about Arabella's charge regarding his family. Drusilla tells him that his parents parted while he was still a baby. His mother drowned herself, and Jude's father brought him up in South Wessex. His father's sister left her husband and went to London with her small daughter, Sue.

At dusk, Jude leaves Drusilla's house. He goes to a frozen pond, and ventures recklessly on to the middle of the ice. Then he goes drinking. On his return home, he finds a note from Arabella saying she has left him. A letter which arrives a few days later explains that she intends to emigrate to Australia with her family. Jude replies that he does not object to her going. He sends her all the money he has and his household goods to be auctioned with those of her family. He takes lodgings in Alfredston. Soon afterwards, he discovers a framed photograph of himself in a pawnbroker's shop.

Returning one evening to the upland, he feels as he did when a boy, before the fateful meeting with Arabella. He is aware that he is near the place where his parents parted. He reads an inscription he had once chiselled on the back of a milestone: 'THITHER J.F.', with a hand pointing towards Christminster. He sees the glow of the town in the distance and resolves to go there as soon as his apprenticeship has ended. He returns to his lodgings, feeling more optimistic, and says his prayers.

Aunt Drusilla repeatedly alludes to flaws and shortcomings which Jude shares with his Fawley ancestors, suggesting his individual fate in marriage is determined in advance by his family's history. Drusilla's belief is grounded in superstition rather than the kind of understanding of inherited characteristics which the modern science of genetics has developed. Nonetheless, we are invited to perceive another determinant of his behaviour over which Jude has no control.

The emigration of Arabella's family to Australia is a dramatic indication of the problems faced by rural communities in the late nineteenth century. Remember that Drusilla considers Christminster remote, although only twenty miles away (see Themes, on Modern Restlessness). The decline of local occupations, such as 'pig-jobbing', reflected the changing nature of the national economy, and was a key factor in the ongoing depopulation of the countryside (see Historical Background, on The Declining Importance of Agriculture).

cotton blower bellows

Bene agere et laetari (Latin) act well and rejoice

Spinoza Baruch Spinoza (1632–77), philosopher

PART SECOND: AT CHRISTMINSTER

Save his own soul he hath no star from 'Prelude' (1871) by Algernon Charles Swinburne (1837–1909)

Notitiam primosque ... 'Nearness produced gradual acquaintance; Time produced love', from *Metamorphoses* IV, by the Roman poet Ovid

CHAPTER 1   Jude moves to Christminster and explores the city at night

Three years later, Jude heads for Christminster, hoping to fulfil the aspirations that had fired his imagination as a boy. After taking inexpensive lodgings in a suburb, he explores the city at night, roaming amongst medieval college buildings. Eventually, after his musings have been interrupted by a policeman, Jude returns to his lodgings and reads before going to sleep. Next morning his thoughts turn to Phillotson, and more fervently to his cousin Sue.

The policeman who interrupts Jude's musings embodies the law; in other words, he represents the curbing of individual freedom by social regulation. In Part First, Chapter 5, a policeman cautions Jude against reading while driving a delivery cart. In Part Sixth, Chapter 1, another policeman intervenes when Jude is addressing a crowd attending a procession of university dons. In each case, the law appears hostile to Jude's aspiration to a scholarly life.

Jude's imagination peoples the deserted nocturnal streets of Christminster with ghostly figures, the spirits of his intellectual heroes.

They are so real to Jude that he speaks aloud to them. These imagined presences form a striking contrast to Arabella's coarse physicality (see Themes, on Ideal Forms & Material Reality).

Dick Whittington mayor of London (d.1423), according to legend, a poor orphan, summoned by bells to fulfil his destiny

Beersheba in Genesis 16:12, a wilderness where Abraham's mistress Hagar wandered with her outcast son Ishmael

the friend and eulogist of Shakespeare Ben Jonson (1572–1637), poet and dramatist

Tractarian member of a movement whose *Tracts for the Times* (1833–41) sought to revitalise the Anglican Church

the Corn Law convert Sir Robert Peel (1788–1850), who sought repeal of the protectionist Corn Laws

the sly author of the immortal Chapter on Christianity Edward Gibbon (1737–94) in Chapter XV of *The Decline and Fall of the Roman Empire* (1776–88)

the poet, the last of the optimists Robert Browning (1812–89), poet

the author of the *Apologia* John Henry Newman (1801–90), whose autobiography was entitled *Apologia Pro Vita Sua* (1864)

the genial Spectator Joseph Addison (1672–1719), essayist. The quotation is taken from *Spectator* No. 26

a gentle-voiced prelate Bishop Thomas Ken (1637–1711)

CHAPTER 2 **Jude finds employment as a stonemason. His thoughts turn to his cousin Sue Bridehead, and to his former schoolmaster, Richard Phillotson**

Jude finds work amongst the stonemasons of Christminster. He writes to great-aunt Drusilla for a photograph of his cousin, Sue Bridehead. She sends one, but insists that Jude should not contact Sue, as that would sully the family name. Jude envisages Phillotson as a reverend parson, and feels himself too 'raw and unpolished' to visit such a refined man (p. 85). After working all day, Jude spends his nights studying, although unable to afford fuel or much food.

Jude discovers Sue working as a decorative painter in a shop selling ecclesiastical artefacts. A few weeks later, he sees her pass by while he is helping to move a block of worked stone.

Sue Bridehead and Richard Phillotson are aligned in Jude's mind as superior creatures, yet when they are later joined in marriage Jude cannot come to terms with their alliance. He is comfortable with idealised conceptions, but deeply troubled by physical realities (see Themes, on Ideal Forms & Material Reality).

He is drawn to Sue's daintiness, which contrasts with his rough working-man's appearance, and he senses the distaste she would feel at his marriage to Arabella. Sue's 'half-visionary form' (p. 90) seems to offer the prospect of reconciling Jude's higher aspirations with his sexual nature.

ogee dome the dome of the cathedral, ornamented with ogee mouldings, formed by two continuous curves in an S-shape
'For wisdom is a defence ...' Ecclesiastes 7:12

CHAPTER 3   **Jude falls in love with Sue. Sue buys statuettes of pagan deities**

Next Sunday, Jude goes to church, hoping to see Sue. He is disappointed in the morning, but in the afternoon she arrives. He is acutely aware of her presence and of his burgeoning love for her.

Not long before this day, Sue had walked into the countryside, reading a book. She met a foreign man, sorting plaster statuettes, some representing Greek deities. She bought images of Venus and Apollo, but became self-conscious with regard to their nakedness, and parcelled them in vegetation before returning to Christminster. At her lodgings, she felt embarrassed by the figures. As she was wrapping them in brown paper, Sue was interrupted by her pious landlady and employer, Miss Fontover. Flustered, Sue pretended that they were statuettes of St Peter and St Mary Magdalen.

Before going to bed, Sue examined her new acquisitions, placing them on her chest-of-drawers, a candle beside each. She had a disturbed night and at one point heard the church clock, heard also by Jude, hard at his studies elsewhere in the city.

When Jude met Arabella Donn, her coarse physical nature contrasted to his unworldly interests and aspirations. Sue Bridehead, on the other hand, appears an almost ethereal creature when compared to his appearance as a manual labourer. Her refined sensitivity places her at the opposite extreme to Arabella in terms of temperament. Thomas Hardy's characterisation has a schematic quality, artificially contrived to produce telling contrasts (see Characterisation).

The picture is complicated by an additional contrast between Jude's Christian piety and the inclination to a pagan understanding which both women show. Arabella's attitudes suggest an affinity with pre-Christian practices of nature worship and fertility rites, an immensely practical religion imbedded in the daily demands of country living. Sue, on the other hand, is a modern city-dweller who has developed a sceptical view of Christianity through her reading. She is drawn to the beliefs and philosophies of ancient Greek civilisation. This set of contrasts has been carefully contrived by Thomas Hardy. He is not simply depicting the course of individual lives, but is writing about a phase of history where the authority of orthodox Christianity is waning (see Themes, on Relativism).

the dew of Hermon   reference to Psalm 133

as distinctly from Cyprus as from Galilee   Cyprus was the centre for worship of Venus, Galilee for worship of Jesus Christ

Julian the Apostate   in the fourth century, Emperor Julian renounced Christian belief and inaugurated a new pagan era

Thou hast conquered, O pale Galilean   from Swinburne's dramatic monologue 'Hymn to Proserpine' (1866), reflecting the last words of Julian the Apostate

All hemin eis Theos ... autou   (Greek) I Corinthians 8:6 'But to us there is but one God, the Father, of whom are all things, and we in him; and one Lord Jesus Christ, by whom are all things, and we by him'

CHAPTER 4   **Jude meets Sue. They visit Richard Phillotson and it is arranged that Sue should become his teaching assistant**

Jude, working in a church, attends a brief Anglican service. Sue is also a member of the small congregation. Jude feels his attraction to her intensify.

Sue visits the stonemason's yard and asks for Jude. He is absent, but learning of the visit he resolves to call on her. A note from Sue, left at his lodgings, says she has learnt of his presence in the city and would like to meet him. She plans to leave Christminster soon. Jude sends a note offering to meet her that evening.

Jude speaks to Sue of Phillotson and his aspirations. Sue tells Jude that she has directed books to a man of that name, but he is merely a village schoolmaster. Jude cannot believe that his old friend has made no further advance towards his goal. They visit Phillotson in Lumsdon, and Jude notes the schoolmaster's careworn appearance. Phillotson requires prompting before he is able to recollect dimly his former pupil. He claims to be comfortable in his current circumstances, but he needs to engage an assistant teacher.

On their way home, Sue tells Jude that Miss Fontover has deliberately broken her statuettes. Sue has determined to find a more independent way to live. Jude promises to speak to Phillotson about appointing Sue as his teaching assistant. He does so the following evening, assuring Phillotson that Sue has previous experience and is keen to make teaching her profession. A suitable arrangement is made.

Jude's interest in Sue is 'unmistakably of a sexual kind' (p. 97), but after his unhappy relationship with the sensual Arabella he seeks to play down that element of physical attraction. He tells himself that his desire for Sue is 'partly a wish for intellectual sympathy, and a craving for loving-kindness in my solitude' (p. 98). Jude's perception of others is filtered through his sense of himself and of his aspirations.

Pusey Edward Bouverie Pusey (1800–82), professor of Hebrew who succeeded Cardinal Newman as leader of the Oxford movement

Ward W.G. Ward (1812–82), religious essayist

Keble John Keble (1792–1866), country clergyman and nonresident professor of poetry at Oxford

CHAPTER 5   Sue accompanies Phillotson to Christminster with a party of schoolchildren. They encounter Jude at an exhibition. Both men are in love with Sue. Later in the week, Jude is appalled to witness Phillotson walking with Sue, his arm around her waist

Sue has taken lodgings in an old house opposite Phillotson's new home, and has started teaching at his school. He gives her private lessons in the evening, in the presence of her landlady Mrs Hawes. They take a party of schoolchildren to a Christminster exhibition to see a model of Jerusalem. Sue questions its authenticity and suggests that Jerusalem compares unfavourably to other cities of the ancient world, such as Athens, Rome and Alexandria. Jude happens to be present. Both he and Phillotson have fallen in love with Sue.

The following day, Phillotson is surprised to discover that Sue has drawn from memory upon her blackboard an aerial view of Jerusalem. Two days later, a school inspector pays a surprise visit. Sue is anxious at the prospect of being observed, and remains shaken after the inspector's departure. Phillotson takes her to his room, gives her brandy to steady her nerves, holds her hand, and tells her she is the best teacher he has ever employed.

On Friday evening, Jude pays an eager visit to Sue. It is wet and gloomy, and he sees Phillotson, carrying an umbrella, walking with his arm around Sue's waist. Jude is sickened by this turn of events, especially as Phillotson is so much older than Sue. He returns to Christminster.

Point of view plays an important role in Thomas Hardy's approach to characterisation. Jude places Sue upon a pedestal, and views her in ideal terms; Phillotson, although impressed by Sue's cleverness, addresses her as 'my dear little girl' (p. 108). The reality of Sue's character does not match the version which either man projects on to her (see Characterisation).

Jude and Phillotson both conceive the course of their future lives in terms of progression towards identifiable goals, but the narrative follows a far more tangled course. Consequences of actions are invariably not those envisaged by the characters, and the momentum of events often veers beyond their control. Conversing with Jude and Phillotson at the exhibition, Sue 'had not the least conception how the hearts of the twain went out to her'; she was unaware 'what a complication she was building up' in the lives of both men (p. 107).

Jude's ambitions are frustrated by unforeseen consequences, and when, with hindsight, he is able to see what has followed from his actions, the painfulness of his situation is intensified: 'The ironical clinch to his sorrow was given by the thought that the intimacy between his cousin and the schoolmaster had been brought about entirely by himself (p. 109).

H.M. Inspector Her Majesty's Inspector, appointed by the Department of Education, under the Education Act of 1870
Mount Moriah the site of Solomon's temple
the Valley of Jehoshaphat valley next to the Mount of Olives
the City of Zion King David's city
Calvary site of Christ's crucifixion
Mount of Olives site of Christ's agony before the crucifixion

CHAPTER 6 **Jude visits great-aunt Drusilla, who is ill. Later, he writes to the college authorities seeking advice on gaining entry to the university. He is advised to resign himself to his lot as a working man**

On the following Sunday, Jude, primarily to avoid contact with Sue or Phillotson, visits aunt Drusilla, who is unwell. Sue was born in the room where the old woman now lies ill. Drusilla cautions against Jude becoming involved with Sue.

Jude meets some villagers in the street. They ask him about Christminster. He confesses that lack of money has prevented him attending the university. Later, Jude writes to college officials requesting advice on gaining admission. After discovering that he will need to save for fifteen years to be able to afford entry to a college, he gazes longingly at those academic buildings from which he seems destined to remain excluded. He thinks his plight might have been bearable with Sue as his companion. Jude has learnt that Phillotson is moving to a larger school in Mid-Wessex, and wonders what this implies for Sue.

Returning home, after drinking, he finds a letter from the master of a college, advising him to settle for his lot as a working man. He goes out and drinks more. Later, he writes in chalk a sardonic quotation from the Book of Job upon the wall of the college which has rejected him.

In the next chapter we are told that Drusilla's life has been 'a struggle with material things' (p. 124). Here she remarks disapprovingly that as children both Sue and Jude were prone to project imaginatively beyond the physical realities of life, 'seeming to see things in the air' (p. 112) (see Themes, on Ideal Forms & Material Reality).

In the preceding chapter, the differing **points of view** from which Jude and Phillotson regard Sue are disclosed. Drusilla views her from another angle, criticising the 'tight strained nerves' and 'impertinence' which characterised Sue when a child (p. 110). Sensitivity, rebelliousness and vivid imagination remain constituents of Sue's personality, but Jude, Phillotson and Drusilla interpret these aspects of her in differing ways from their various points of view.

Jude's intellectual heroes are writers who have transmitted their ideas to future generations through print. Here Jude responds to rejection by writing upon a wall in chalk, an impermanent medium that will soon fade. He also falls back on biblical text, rather than formulating some original statement.

'Excelsior' poem by Henry Wadsworth Longfellow (1807–82)

'There was a sound of revelry by night' reference to *Childe Harold's Pilgrimage*, Canto III (1816), by George Gordon, Lord Byron (1788–1824)

Poe's 'Raven' 'The Raven', a poem by Edgar Allen Poe (1809–49)

Crusoe *Robinson Crusoe* (1719), a novel by Daniel Defoe (1660–1731)

Heine Heinrich Heine (1797–1856), German poet

CHAPTER 7   **Jude gets drunk. He is dismissed from his job and returns to Marygreen, feeling a failure. A curate advises Jude that he might still become a preacher**

Next morning, Jude, depressed after reading again the letter from the college, heads for a Christminster tavern. He discusses his frustrated aspirations with some of the regular clientele. After reciting the Creed in Latin, he calls the assembled company fools, and departs, slamming the door behind him.

That night he visits Sue in Lumsdon and pours out his sorrows. Then he sleeps till dawn when, overcome by shame, he leaves noiselessly. Returning to his lodgings, he discovers that he has been dismissed from his job on account of absence. He walks to Drusilla's house in Marygreen. After sleeping, he awakens with an oppressive sense of failure.

Jude speaks with a curate who has come to pray with his aunt. He says that he no longer cares for social success, but regrets he will never become an ordained minister. The curate tells Jude that a man of his sincerity and educational attainment might still enter the Church as a licensed preacher.

Although Jude appears to be aware that 'drinking was the regular, stereotyped resource of the despairing worthless' (p. 71), he does not have the strength of will to refrain. His attraction to alcohol as a form of 'self-extermination' (p. 70) foreshadows Sue's later acts of self-denial, and the suicide of Little Father Time.

Thomas Hardy's use of telling contrasts to further characterisation extends to his portrayal of the group of undergraduates drinking in the tavern. They are interested in dogs, and have no knowledge of Latin. Their boorish indifference to scholarship contrasts with Jude's keenness to learn, and their privileged status contrasts with his exclusion from Christminster's centres of learning.

Credo in unum Deum ... (Latin) 'I believe in one God, the Father almighty, Maker of heaven and earth, of all things visible and invisible'

Crucifixus etiam pro nobis ... (Latin) 'Crucified also for us, suffered under Pontius Pilate, and was buried'

the Nicene ... the Apostles Christian creeds, or statements of belief

Et unam Catholicam ... (Latin) 'And in one Holy, Catholic, and Apostolic Church. I confess one Baptism for the remission of sins. And I expect the Resurrection of the dead, and Life Everlasting. Amen'

the Ratcatcher's Daughter popular Victorian ballad recounting a lover's suicide

Laocoon Roman sculpture representing a Trojan priest and his two sons being crushed by serpents

Part third: at Melchester

SAPPHO Sappho, Greek poet (seventh century BC)

CHAPTER 1   **Jude plans to become a curate. Sue is admitted to a training-school for teachers. Jude visits her in Melchester and she announces her intention to marry Phillotson. Jude finds work renovating the cathedral**

Changing course from 'the intellectual and emulative life' to 'the ecclesiastical and altruistic life' (p. 129), Jude now aspires to become a poor yet pious curate.

A letter from Sue announces that she has won a scholarship to attend a training-school for teachers in Melchester. Jude conceives the plan of working as a stonemason in Melchester, while preparing for theological college. He hopes to commence his ministry at the age of thirty, as Jesus did.

After Christmas, a letter from Sue tells him she is lonely and miserable. She now resents Phillotson's advice to train as a teacher. Jude heads to Melchester and finds Sue subdued, but less despondent than her letter suggested. She describes bitterly the disappointments of her new life.

Jude and Sue hold hands. Sue discloses that she has agreed to marry Phillotson in two years' time, when she has qualified as a teacher. Jude says her engagement will make no difference to their friendship. Sue says 'What does it matter about what one is going to do two years hence!' (p. 134). Jude comments on the modernness of Sue's thinking. She replies: 'I am more ancient than medievalism, if you only knew' (p. 135).

Jude manages to find employment, eventually becoming involved in renovation of the cathedral.

> Jude hopes to commence his ministry at the age of thirty, and consoles himself with the thought that Jesus established a precedent for that. Copious allusions to the Bible reflect the extent of Jude and Sue's exposure to Christian scriptures as they grew up, but it also heightens the **irony** of their departure from orthodox belief. Jude finds consolation in the sense that he is following Christ's example. Later, Sue finds a comparable religious context for her own self-sacrificing tendencies.
>
> **coup de grâce** (French: a stroke of mercy) a final or decisive action

Paley and Butler William Paley (1743–1805), author of *Evidences of Christianity* (1794); Joseph Butler (1692–1752), author of *The Analogy of Religion* (1736)

CHAPTER 2   **Returning from a day's outing, Jude and Sue stay overnight at a shepherd's cottage**

A few weeks later, Jude and Sue visit Wardour Castle and its picture galleries. Afterwards, they walk seven miles to another railway station, in order to follow an alternative route to Melchester. Sue grows weary. They rest at a cottage belonging to a shepherd and his mother. The shepherd advises they will not be able to catch their train in time, so they accept his offer to stay overnight at his cottage.

Sue speaks of her own unconventionality; Jude is not convinced that she is unorthodox. Next morning, they catch a train to Melchester. Jude accompanies Sue to the training-college, and before they part she gives him a new photograph of herself.

The narrator observes: 'His Sue's conduct was one lovely conundrum to him; he could say no more' (p. 136). The possessive pronoun 'his' suggests ownership, which proves **ironic** as Sue is not readily amenable to the conventional middle-class Victorian perception of a wife as her husband's property. Indeed, she is unable to enter into a contract of marriage with Jude. The pronoun additionally suggests that Jude has his own distinct perception of Sue. She remains a riddle and a puzzle to Jude and to Phillotson.

Sue is dressed with 'a nunlike simplicity of costume that was enforced rather than desired' (p. 136). Towards the end of the novel, Sue shifts her position from pagan sceptic to pious Christian, and assumes chaste dress as a matter of choice.

The shepherd, like Drusilla, speaks Wessex **dialect** (see Language & Style).

Photographs play a significant role in *Jude the Obscure* (see Textual Analysis, Text 2).

Wardour Castle eighteenth-century castle near Shaftesbury (Shaston), well-known for its collection of Italian art

Fonthill Fonthill Abbey, in Wiltshire, built in pseudo-Gothic style by the writer William Beckford (1759–1844)

Del Sarto Andrea Del Sarto, Italian painter (1486–1531)

Guido Reni Italian painter (1575–1642)

Spagnoletto Italian painter (1588–1652)

Sassoferrato Italian painter (1605–85)

Carlo Dolci Italian painter (1616–86)

Lely Sir Peter Lely, English painter (1618–80)

Reynolds Sir Joshua Reynolds, English painter (1723–92)

CHAPTER 3   Sue is placed in solitary confinement following her absence from the training-school. She escapes and takes refuge with Jude

Sue's overnight absence from the training-school is spotted by one of the mistresses. On her return, Sue is confined to solitary quarters for a week. Other students protest, expressing their solidarity with Sue. Sue manages to escape. In doing so she crosses a river, and is cold and wet when she arrives at Jude's lodgings. Sue sits by the fire, wearing Jude's Sunday suit and great-coat. He gives her brandy in water, and then she sleeps.

In this chapter, Sue expresses sentiments which suggest a feminist orientation (see Contemporary Approaches, Feminist). She speaks of her clothes as 'sexless cloth and linen' (p. 145) suggesting that the association of dress with gender is determined by convention rather than intrinsic properties of the fabric.

Yet in contradiction to this view of gender construction according to social convention, we are told that every face in the training-school bears 'the legend "the Weaker" upon it, as the penalty of the sex wherein they were moulded, which by no possible exertion of their willing hearts and abilities could be made strong while the inexorable laws of nature remain what they are' (p. 141). We may perceive **irony** in this assertion that women are naturally weaker than men. Jude's personal weaknesses are regularly displayed, and he fails to acquire even a modicum of social power. In the next chapter, complicating matters, Jude feels that Sue's 'very helplessness seemed to make her so much stronger than he' (p. 150).

CHAPTER 4   **Sue stays overnight at Jude's lodgings and tells him**
             about her past life and her current beliefs

Sue stays the night in Jude's room. She talks again of her
unconventionality and refers to her extensive reading. She tells Jude about
her close friendship with a Christminster undergraduate. They lived
together in London, in one room, but Sue remained chaste as she did not
feel love for him. He died young, and she has been troubled by a guilty
sense that his death was hastened by her inability to love him.

Sue's father refused to allow her to return home, so she moved to
Christminster, where Jude met her. She speaks of her atheism, and Jude
is shocked. She is also disrespectful towards the Christminster scholars,
pointing to the injustice of Jude's exclusion, while those with wealth but
none of Jude's passion for learning are admitted. She steers the
conversation away from discussion of her life with Phillotson.

Sue wishes to rearrange Jude's copy of the New Testament, as she
has modified her own. He senses that her revisions might be sacrilegious,
and talks instead of his personal feelings for her.

Next morning, her clothes are dry. Jude washes in the yard.

Social construction of gender is again an issue. Sue asserts that she
has mixed with men 'almost as one of their own sex. I mean I have
not felt about them as most women are taught to feel' (p. 147). She
is affirming that emotional responses may be the product of
education rather than evidence of a fixed human nature.

Sue goes against the grain of conventional moral wisdom at the
time, which established demarcation of many activities into
separate social spheres, in order to safeguard the respectability of
both men and women. She and the Christminster undergraduate
used to go about together 'like two men almost' (p. 148). Sue is
signalling her commitment to unorthodox behaviour, even though
the word 'almost', occurring in this and the previous quotation,
suggests there are conventional limits which Sue has not passed.
She later admits that she does not always have the courage of her
convictions.

Sue remained self-consciously chaste with this man, and that
foreshadows her resistance to sexual contact with Phillotson and

with Jude. Psychological literary criticism would seek to explain the oddities and contradictions in Sue's behaviour with reference to her repression of sexual impulses (see Contemporary Approaches, Psychological).

Lemprière John Lemprière, English classical scholar (1765–1824)

Catullus Roman poet (*c*.84–*c*.54BC)

Martial Roman writer (40–102)

Juvenal Roman satirist (*c*.60–*c*.130)

Lucian Greek satirist (second century AD)

Beaumont and Fletcher Francis Beaumont (1584–1616) and John Fletcher (1579–1625), collaborating English playwrights

Boccaccio Giovanni Boccaccio, Italian author of *The Decameron* (1313–75)

Scarron Paul Scarron, French poet and satirist (1610–60)

De Brantôme Pierre de Bourdeilles de Brantôme, French historian (*c*.1540–1614)

Sterne Laurence Sterne, Anglo-Irish novelist (1713–68)

De Foe Daniel Defoe, English writer (1660–1731)

Smollett Tobias Smollett, Scottish novelist (1721–71)

Fielding Henry Fielding, English novelist (1707–54)

'twitched the robe ...' from Robert Browning's poem 'Too Late' (1864)

'O ghastly glories of saints' from Swinburne's poem 'Hymn to Proserpine' (1866)

Voltairean adjective from 'Voltaire', pseudonym of François-Marie Arouet, French satirist (1694–1778)

Ganymedes physically beautiful cup-bearer to Zeus

CHAPTER 5   **Sue stays at a school run by a friend's sister. Jude visits her and learns that the training-school has refused to readmit her**

Sue visits a friend's sister, who runs a school near Shaston, eighteen miles away. Jude accompanies her to the station. As they part, she tells Jude not to love her. He is gloomy but next morning he receives a letter confirming her arrival, and granting him permission to love her. He writes, asking if he may visit. There is no reply, so he travels to the school, and finds her ill with a cold. The authorities at the training-school refuse to re-admit her, and advise that she and Jude should marry as soon as possible.

Aspects of Sue's character are given further exposure in this chapter. She cherishes a sense of her autonomy, yet she is impulsive, and can respond with confusion to unforeseen consequences of her actions. Jude has come to regard Sue as 'rather unreasonable, not to say capricious (p. 159).

CHAPTER 6 **Phillotson now runs a school in Shaston. He discovers that Sue has been expelled from the training-school and is living with Jude. Jude reveals to Sue his marriage to Arabella**

Richard Phillotson has returned to Shaston, his home town, where he now runs a large school for boys. He has agreed to Sue's request not to visit her at the training-school, but that request disconcerts him as his sights are firmly set on marriage to her. He pays a surprise visit to Melchester and learns of her expulsion. Bewildered, Phillotson enters the cathedral and notices Jude amongst the workers repairing it. Jude, awaiting Sue's arrival, tells Phillotson how she came to live with him. He takes pains to stress her innocence.

Sue does not arrive at the cathedral, and Jude later meets her by chance. She is irritable after retrieving her things from the training-school. She is considerably more upset when Jude tells her of his marriage to Arabella. He says that aunt Drusilla had warned him he was not suited for marriage. Sue says that her father had told her the same thing. They part on better terms, but Jude feels that he does not understand Sue.

The horizon of Phillotson's aspirations has contracted to match his material circumstances. Instead of looking to the future he has turned to history, developing his interest in Roman-Britannic antiquities. Interpretation of Sue's motives is still more compelling study for him. He ponders on her photograph, a duplicate of one Jude owns. But in this novel, reading motivation and predicting responses are highly problematic activities, especially with regard to Sue, who is variously described as a conundrum, a riddle and a puzzle.

Sue is keen to affirm that human relationships can have a strong basis beyond sexual attraction, and she is critical of people who are incapable of recognising this: 'Their philosophy only recognizes relations based on animal desire. The wide field of strong attachment where desire plays, at least, only a secondary part, is ignored by them' (pp. 167–8). The intensity of Sue's feeling seems to be determined, in part at least, by her own distaste for 'animal desire' (see Contemporary Approaches, Psychological).

CHAPTER 7 **Jude receives a letter from Sue announcing her imminent marriage to Phillotson, and asking Jude to give her away. The ceremony takes place**

A few days later, Jude is overwhelmed by a letter, signed formally with Sue's full name, announcing her imminent marriage to Phillotson. She complains that the Church views her as an object to be given 'like a she-ass or she-goat, or any other domestic animal' (p. 170). She asks Jude, as a married relative, to give her away. He reluctantly agrees, and moves into larger quarters, suitable for preliminaries to the wedding.

Sue arrives in Melchester ten days before the ceremony and stays in the same house as Jude, but on another floor. On the day of the wedding they have breakfast together. Then they visit the church. Leaving it, they encounter Phillotson. Sue tells him she and Jude have been rehearsing. After the ceremony, all three share a simple meal at Jude's lodgings. On her departure, Sue appears anxious.

Sue eagerly detects correspondences between men and women, in order to affirm her ability to enter into conventionally masculine pursuits. Jude, on the other hand, notes differences between the sexes, trying to understand how Sue can act in ways which would not occur to him: 'Women were different from men in such matters. Was it that they were, instead of more sensitive, as reputed, more callous, and less romantic; or were they more heroic?' (p. 174).

to play the Spartan the citizens of Sparta, in ancient Greece, were renowned for their discipline and courage

'... I can find no way' from Robert Browning's poem 'The Worst of It'

CHAPTER 8   Jude suggests that Sue should visit their aunt Drusilla, who is dying. He meets Arabella at an inn, and they spend the night in Aldbrickham

Sue and Phillotson spend their honeymoon in London.

After visiting Marygreen, Jude sends a message telling Sue that their aunt Drusilla is dying. He suggests that Sue should visit the old woman the following evening.

Jude is offered work by his old employer but he finds it impossible to stay in 'this place of vanished dreams' (p. 178). Depressed, he goes to an inn and drinks. There he encounters Arabella, working as a barmaid. She left Australia three months previously. They arrange to meet at nine o'clock, precluding the meeting Jude has arranged with Sue.

Arabella offers to visit Jude's dying aunt with him the following afternoon, and he agrees to this arrangement. They go to Aldbrickham and stay at an inn.

In spite of Jude's firm declaration 'I am as I was' (p. 181), he responds, mentally and physically, to changing circumstances. Now, when he visits Christminster, he is haunted by memories of Sue rather than by visions of intellectual heroes who once exercised his imagination. This illustrates how **point of view** may change according to experience (see Themes, on Relativism).

It is indicative of his waning faith in a caring God that Jude senses the universe's indifference to his own plight and to human affairs more generally. He has grown acutely aware of 'the scorn of Nature for man's finer emotions, and her lack of interest in his aspirations' (p. 177). He nonetheless clings to the belief that there is some kind of ordered intention in the world. It is characteristic of both Jude and Sue to imagine some large force at work, whether it be called Nature, Fate, Nemesis, or Necessity. Arabella attends to the specifics of relationships, while they envisage the abstract.

Old-Midsummer eve   24 June, around the time of the summer solstice

CHAPTER 9   After parting from Arabella, Jude chances to meet Sue.
             They visit aunt Drusilla

Next morning, Jude and Arabella return to Christminster by train.
Arabella reveals that she has married again in Australia. She and Jude
have resolved nothing, and after their parting Jude feels degraded by
renewed contact with her. By chance he meets Sue, who has been worried
about him. They walk to Alfredston, passing the cottage where Jude and
Arabella had spent their married days, and they cross the field where Jude
as a boy was beaten for neglecting his bird-scaring duties.

They arrive at their aunt's cottage. Drusilla tells Sue that she, like
Jude, will rue the day that she marries. Her dismissive comments
concerning Phillotson upset Sue, who leaves the room. Jude follows. Sue
departs for Shaston, telling Jude not to visit her for a while. At
Marygreen, Jude receives a letter sent by Arabella from London, where
she has joined her Australian husband to run a public house. She has
written to say goodbye.

Characterisation is again developed by contrast, with Jude
positioned schematically between Sue's ethereal character and
Arabella's earthiness. Sue's physical presence seems to Jude so
tenuous that he is struck at times by the impossibility of her being
'a human wife to any average man' (p. 187). She assumes, in Jude's
understanding, the quality of an ideal form, adrift in the material
world (see Themes, on Ideal Forms & Material Reality).

Jude has come under the influence of Sue's unorthodox views
regarding the effects of social institutions upon individual lives.
This is evident in his observation: 'Wifedom has not yet annihilated
and digested you in its vast maw as an atom which has no further
individuality' (p. 189). Rejecting social conventions, they
nonetheless remain subject to the conventional judgements of
others, and they soon come under the harsh glare of hostile public
scrutiny.

Sebastiano's Lazarus a painting, *Resurrection of Lazarus* (1518), by
Sebastiano Del Piombo (1485–1547)
the Ascetics of the second century self-denying hermits, including St Antony
(250–*c*.350); precursors of the monastic life

chapter 10   Jude visits the composer of a hymn, expecting a
person of spiritual integrity. He finds instead a man
driven by need for money

Jude returns to Melchester, and to religious study. He also practises
reading music, and joins a choir. Jude determines to meet a local man,
who has written a hymn he finds emotionally affecting. He visits him in
Kennetbridge, but the composer loses interest in Jude when he discovers
that he is poor. He says he is giving up music for the wine trade, where
there is money to be made.

Back in Melchester, he finds an invitation to dine with Sue, who
now regrets her lapse into conventionality. But the designated hour had
passed while Jude was on his expedition to Kennetbridge. He ardently
requests another invitation, but Sue has again become more prudent. A
meeting is arranged for the Thursday preceding Good Friday.

> Jude has directed his energies to music as a way of preventing a
> lapse into drinking; but the writer of hymns is entering the wine
> business as a consequence of his dissatisfaction with the meagre
> pecuniary rewards of music. The hymn is regarded differently from
> their differing **points of view**. This is a good example of the
> patterned **irony** that structures *Jude the Obscure*. A path which Jude
> hopes will lead to a form of personal salvation is abandoned by
> another character who considers it a dead end and is heading in the
> opposite direction. The novel is filled with such ironic reversals.

Part fourth: at shaston

J. Milton   John Milton (1608–74), poet. The quotation is from his prose
pamphlet, *The Doctrine and Discipline of Divorce* (1643)

chapter 1   Jude meets Sue in the schoolhouse at Shaston

Jude arrives in Shaston. Once the children have left the schoolhouse and
Sue has followed them, Jude enters the empty classroom. He plays the
hymn that has moved him on the piano which Phillotson once stored at
Drusilla's house. Sue enters, and asks him to continue playing. He gets

her to play instead. She stops, and they spontaneously clasp each other's hand.

Old-Grove's Place, her home, depresses her, so they have tea in the schoolhouse. They talk of the Apocryphal gospels, then Jude accuses Sue of sometimes being a flirt. She denies this and, accusing him of cruelty, asks him to leave. But as he departs from the building she detains him, and they talk through an open window. She suggests that sensitive people, such as they are, inevitably suffer, as the social world is unable to accommodate their complex natures. She invites Jude to return a week later.

Jude misses the coach to catch the next train, so he waits in Shaston for the last train to Melchester. He watches Sue inside her house as she looks lovingly at a photograph. She is crying; he is sure it is a photograph of himself. He will not be able to resist visiting her again.

The narrator's account of the history of Shaston foregrounds the processes of change that occur through history. Shaston's picturesqueness is now largely unappreciated; it has become an unvisited town. Crucially, it is not accessible by railway on account of its topography (see Historical Background, on Railways).

Jude's visit to Sue is cast in an **ironic** light by the fact that Shaston was formerly a site of holy pilgrimage. The collective devotion of a pious Christian society is here diminished to one man's obsessive devotion to a woman whom he has come to revere as 'almost a divinity' (p. 145). The narrator remarks that Shaston has 'passed through a curious period of corruption' (p. 200), during which the town's people demonstrated their sense of humour and their taste for sensual pleasure, in stark contrast to Sue's chaste intensity.

Thomas Hardy is portraying a society where forms of almost nomadic wandering are starting to supersede the rootedness of traditional ways of life. A modern phenomenon in Shaston is that it has become headquarters for itinerant showmen who travel to fairs and markets (see Themes, on Modern Restlessness). The uprooting of England's rural population is indicative of changing modes of transportation, changing economic relationships and of widening horizons generating aspirations that lead some rural people, like Jude, to seek another mode of living (see Historical Background, on The Declining Importance of Agriculture).

Palladour the ancient British name for Shaftesbury, on which Shaston is based

Drayton Michael Drayton (1563–1631), poet

King Edward 'the Martyr' ruled England 975–8

the Dissolution of monasteries by Henry VIII between 1536 and 1540

Don Quixote knight in the famous Spanish novel by Miguel de Cervantes (1547–1616)

CHAPTER 2   Aunt Drusilla dies. Following the funeral, Jude and Sue discuss the effect that marriage has had upon their lives

Next morning, Jude receives a note from Sue instructing him not to visit the following week. He replies that he will acquiesce. On Easter Monday, he receives a message from Widow Edlin, saying that aunt Drusilla is dying. He walks to Marygreen, but Drusilla has died before his arrival. He conveys this news to Sue, who attends the funeral. Sue and Jude talk of their aunt's distaste for marriage within their family.

Sue and Jude hold hands, but he tells her that he has no more feelings of love left in him. He discloses that Arabella has returned and that he intends to live with her, but in the way Sue lives with her husband, without real commitment. She is upset at his apparent readiness to return to Arabella, and she speaks of her intense unhappiness with Phillotson. Jude asserts that she would have been his own wife had he not foolishly married Arabella. Sue hurries out to Drusilla's grave, and then proceeds to Widow Edlin's house.

Jude has a sleepless night, disturbed further by the pitiful sound of a trapped rabbit. Jude kills the animal to save it from further suffering. Sue talks to him from her window. He kisses her hand, and declares that he has abandoned his religious beliefs. She admits that before her wedding she had not really considered what marriage actually involved. Weeping, she leans forward and kisses the top of Jude's head. She then closes her window, and Jude returns to his aunt's cottage.

Jude's restless sleep is disturbed by the sound of a rabbit cruelly trapped in a gin. This **image** of a suffering animal recalls

Phillotson's injunction, in the novel's first chapter, that Jude should be kind to other creatures. It also recalls the suffering of the pig which he slaughtered with Arabella in Part First, Chapter 10. But above all the image conveys a sense that Jude himself is a helpless creature trapped by forces beyond his comprehension. In the next chapter, Sue is depicted as an animal trapped in its lair, as she cowers in a closet, hiding from her husband.

Also in the next chapter, Jude, showing increasingly the impact of Sue's influence, considers the harmful effect of social conventions followed blindly and without questioning. He conceives the damage to individual lives **metaphorically**, in terms of traps and snares, and is critical of 'the artificial system of things, under which the normal sex-impulses are turned into devilish domestic gins and springes to noose and hold back those who want to progress' (p. 217).

CHAPTER 3   **Jude and Sue kiss on parting. Sue tells her husband that she wishes to leave him and live with Jude. Phillotson resists this, agreeing instead that he and Sue should live apart, within the same house**

Next morning, Jude and Sue walk to Alfredston. Returning alone an hour later, Jude's face bears 'a look of exaltation not unmixed with recklessness' (p. 216). The couple kissed before parting. He weighs the authority of his long-held religious beliefs against his feelings for Sue. At dusk, in his garden, he burns his formerly cherished volumes of theology and ethics.

Sue, meanwhile, has determined to shun Jude and make him suffer. Her husband meets her at Shaston station, and she tells him that she has allowed Jude to hold her hand, but does not mention the kiss. Later that night, Phillotson, preoccupied with matters of school administration, talks to his wife as he prepares for bed. Sue, however, is not in the room. She is downstairs, ostensibly reading. Later, Phillotson discovers she has locked herself inside a clothes-closet beneath the stairs. Sue is hiding, unable to bear contact with him.

Over breakfast, she expresses her wish to live apart from Phillotson. He says she is committing a sin in not liking her husband. She replies that she does like him, but considers it adulterous to live with him without feeling any physical attraction. She implores him to be her friend and have pity on her. She then reveals that she plans to live with Jude.

The customary bell summons the couple to school. Written notes pass between them as they teach. Sue insists on the seriousness of her request. Phillotson refuses to sanction her living disreputably with Jude. Sue replies that respectability is not important to her. Phillotson asks for time to think matters through, in the meantime agreeing that he and Sue should live apart within the same house.

> In conversation with Phillotson, Sue suggests that 'if people are at all peculiar in character they have to suffer from the very rules that produce comfort in others!' (p. 222). She has jettisoned those conventions of belief and practice by means of which past societies have managed to achieve a workable reconciliation between personal inclinations and universal conditions. She laments the cruelty of the universe, which she blames for her personal unhappiness. Her rejection of conventional behaviour and of past systems for organising human society leaves her reliant upon the unpredictable and volatile life of her instincts as a measure of what is right.

> Phillotson finds Sue 'puzzling and unpredictable' (p. 224), and is critical of her 'eccentricities'. He laments, 'There's no order or regularity in your sentiments!' (p. 221). But the novel also exposes the inadequacy of conventional thinking, such as Phillotson's, especially in relation to the institution of marriage. Sue's rebellion against unjust conditions may be seen as perfectly justifiable (see Contemporary Approaches, Feminist). But while her horizons had been expanded and her expectations raised by changing views during the second half of the nineteenth century, the means to make practical changes to improve the lives of women like herself were not available to her (see Themes, on Individual Lives & Historical Periods).

> Novelists during the early decades of the twentieth century continued to reflect this transitional aspect of the age. It produced, for example, the anxious, introspective narratives of Virginia Woolf (1882–1941).

ipso facto (Latin) 'by the deed itself'

Jeremy Taylor (1613–67), Anglican clergyman and writer

Doddridge Philip Doddridge (1702–51), nonconformist minister and writer

a whited sepulchre reference to Matthew 23:27, signifying hypocrisy

J.S. Mill's words from *On Liberty* (1859) by John Stuart Mill (1806–73)

argumentum ad verecundiam (Latin) 'appeal to one's modesty'

Humboldt from *The Sphere and Duties of Government* (1792; trans. 1854) by Wilhelm von Humboldt (1767–1835)

CHAPTER 4   **Phillotson enters his old bedroom by mistake, and disturbs Sue who responds by leaping from a window. Phillotson confides in his friend Gillingham. Phillotson consents to Sue's departure, and she leaves Shaston**

After studying Roman antiquities until two in the morning, Phillotson absentmindedly goes to the bedroom he formerly shared with Sue. She starts wildly from her bed and leaps from a window. Phillotson retrieves her from the gravel outside, dazed but not physically injured. Phillotson retires alone to his room, feeling sickened that she finds him repugnant.

The following evening, Phillotson walks to the small town of Leddenton, to visit Gillingham, a friend and fellow schoolteacher. Phillotson confides that Sue feels strong aversion to him and loves someone else. He accepts responsibility for an ill-judged marriage to an innocent young woman, but remarks that she is more intelligent than he. He tells of Sue's leap from the window and concludes that he will let her go, following instinct rather than judgement.

Phillotson reveals that he overheard the conversation between Sue and Jude in the schoolhouse. He believes their love is pure and will endure. Gillingham warns that such an attitude might lead to 'a general domestic disintegration. The family would no longer be the social unit' (p. 231). He accompanies Phillotson a few miles towards Shaston, expressing hope that their renewed acquaintance might be sustained. He suggests that Sue 'ought to be smacked, and brought to her senses' (p. 232).

Next morning, Phillotson consents unconditionally to Sue's departure. Some days later, they eat their last meal together. Sue is nervous, aware of the pain she is inflicting. Phillotson consolingly suggests he is a bachelor by nature. He will immerse himself in writing about the Roman antiquities of Wessex. Sue offers to help copy the manuscript, as a friend. Phillotson says he prefers to have no further contact, or even knowledge of her future actions.

He watches from an upstairs window, until he can no longer hear the wheels of the omnibus that carries her to the station. He then walks a mile in that direction before returning home, where he finds Gillingham awaiting him. Phillotson reveals that his wife has gone to join her lover. Gillingham helps Phillotson pack away things Sue has left behind.

The revival of Phillotson's friendship with Gillingham may heighten our sense of Jude's isolation, when apart from Arabella and Sue. It also serves a useful technical function. The dialogue between them in effect externalises Phillotson's internal debate concerning his relationship with Sue. Gillingham acts as a sounding-board, offering conventional patriarchal responses to Phillotson's bewildered musings about his young wife. The conversation is staged by Thomas Hardy to enable us to follow the line of thought which leads Phillotson to relinquish his wife to her cousin.

Phillotson gives us a sense of Sue's intensity, saying that 'her intellect sparkles like diamonds, while mine smoulders like brown paper', and he conveys her complexity and changeability through the admission: 'She's one too many for me!'. He also remarks upon the closeness of Sue and Jude: 'They seem to be one person split in two!' (p. 229).

The influence of Sue's refusal to follow fixed guidelines seems to have extended to her customarily cautious husband, who declares, 'I simply am going to act by instinct, and let principles take care of themselves' (p. 230). This instinctual response has disastrous consequences. Gillingham, the voice of patriarchal reason, warns that such an unconventional attitude might lead to 'a general domestic disintegration. The family would no longer be the social unit' (p. 231). He advocates the violent reprisal of smacking Sue.

Thomas Hardy shows conflicting points of view, while revealing flaws on both sides of the argument.

Phillotson, again adopting Sue's high seriousness of tone, declares that he finds himself embroiled in 'a daily, continuous tragedy' (p. 231). Is *Jude the Obscure* a tragedy? Or does the intense, anxious self-consciousness of Jude and Sue devalue the tragic to the status of a self-inflicted defeat?

Where Duncliffe ... from 'Shaftesbury Feäir' by Dorsetshire dialect poet William Barnes (1801–86)

Laon and Cynthia actually 'Laon and Cythna' (1818), a poem by Shelley, retitled *The Revolt of Islam*

Paul and Virginia *Paul et Virginie* (1787) by Bernardin de Saint-Pierre (1737–1814)

CHAPTER 5 **Jude meets Sue's train and they proceed to Aldbrickham. They stay at the hotel where Jude has previously stayed with Arabella. Sue discovers this, and is distressed**

A day before leaving Shaston, Sue sent a request that Jude should meet her from the train. On meeting her, he boards the train, with tickets for Aldbrickham, a much larger town where they will be unknown. He reveals that he has agreed to divorce Arabella, so she may legally marry her Australian husband.

They read a note from Phillotson, which acknowledges Jude and Sue's love for one another and instructs him to take care of her. Sue objects when she discovers Jude has booked only one room for them. He suggests she does not love him. She admits that she does not always have the courage to adhere to her unconventional views.

They stay at another hotel. A maid tells Sue she remembers Jude staying there with another woman. Sue discovers that her room is the one in which Jude had spent the night with Arabella following their reunion, and she cries. Jude tells her not to throw a tantrum about nothing, and discloses that Arabella has married again. Jude and Sue are gradually reconciled. She allows him to kiss her on the cheek before he retires to his room.

The coincidence that results in Sue occupying the room which Jude had previously slept in with Arabella is an example of the widespread contrivance Thomas Hardy uses to shape this narrative. Such contrivance may not disrupt credibility in isolated instances, but applied insistently, as it is in *Jude the Obscure*, it foregrounds artifice, and complicates our response to the novel. The novel becomes a highly self-conscious work, patterned and distorted, distinct from literary **realism**, but arguably an appropriate way to tell a story of hypersensitive, intensely self-aware people, such as Jude and Sue.

Jude says to Sue 'under your teaching, I hate convention' (p. 239). He has taken her as his tutor in unorthodox thinking. But as Jude becomes more and more disaffected with conventional beliefs and modes of conduct, Sue starts to show signs that she really needs the context of orthodoxy. Jude is stunned by her timidity in refusing to share a room with him, and he suggests that 'under the affectation of independent views you are as enslaved to the social code as any woman I know!' (p. 241).

Sue admits that she does not in practice have the courage of her convictions, and repeats 'I jumped out of the window' as if to prove her integrity (p. 243). Significantly, that action evaded physical contact with Phillotson, and here she seeks to keep Jude physically apart from her (see Contemporary Approaches, Psychological).

The soldier-saints ... from Robert Browning's poem, 'The Statue and the Bust'

'the shadowy third' from Robert Browning's poem, 'By the Fireside'

Shelley's 'Epipsychidion' poem published in 1821. The title is Greek, meaning 'little soul within a soul'

CHAPTER 6   **Phillotson has to resign from his teaching post, because he consented to Sue's departure to live with Jude**

A month after Sue's departure, the people of Shaston begin to recognise the actual nature of her separation from her husband. Phillotson admits to the chairman of the School Committee that he consented to Sue leaving him for her lover. Phillotson is asked to resign, as he has condoned his wife's adultery. He tells Gillingham that he will not do so, as he is convinced he has acted rightly.

A note of dismissal arrives. Phillotson contests it, arguing that he has acted out of 'natural charity'. The Board insists that as he is a teacher his 'private eccentricities' are a matter of public concern (p. 247). A scuffle breaks out amongst those in attendance, and Phillotson regrets he did not simply resign. In the period which follows, his health deteriorates and he takes to his bed, overwhelmed by a sense of failure.

Gillingham writes an anonymous note telling Sue of her husband's plight. It reaches her by a circuitous route, as he does not know her address. Three days later, Sue visits Phillotson. He says he is going away. She arranges a mirror so he can see the sunset from his bed. Sue lets out that Jude has been married to Arabella, but is soon to be divorced.

Gillingham is outraged by Sue's behaviour; he had anticipated she would return to her husband permanently. Phillotson envisages poverty as his future lot, as he can no longer find work as a teacher. He intends to divorce Sue.

Phillotson is dismissed from his job as a schoolteacher amid scenes of violent unruliness. The event is described as 'farcical yet melancholy' (p. 248). In the chapter before last, Phillotson saw his situation to be **tragic**, now it appears closer to **farce**. Gossip has fuelled his downfall, and the scuffle surrounding his dismissal aligns Phillotson with the itinerant fair and market workers who supported him, against citizens defending their staid respectability. This appears closer to low **comedy** than tragedy.

In the next chapter, talking about his divorce from Arabella, Jude says: 'There is this advantage in being poor obscure people like us – that these things are done for us in a rough and ready fashion'. He goes on to say, 'If we'd been patented nobilities we should have had infinite trouble …' (p. 258). Is it possible for such obscure figures to assume the stature of tragic heroes?

M. Antoninus (Long) the quotation is from *The Thoughts of the Emperor* by Marcus Aurelius Antoninus (121–180), translated by George Long in 1862

CHAPTER 1 **Jude and Sue are divorced from their former partners**

In Aldbrickham, on a Sunday in February, Sue and Jude receive a letter announcing completion of divorce proceedings between Phillotson and Sue. Jude has recently become divorced from Arabella. Later, the couple walk arm-in-arm through the frosty fields. Sue remains fearful of marriage and would prefer to continue living as they have been, sleeping apart. Jude complains that she has never said she loves him.

Sue helps Jude at work, doing lettering for headstones.

> Sue asserts that fewer women than is supposed actually like marriage; they enter into the contract for the social advantage it can bestow. She displays feminist awareness of oppression or exclusion which women experience in this patriarchal society, that functions according to 'iron contract' and 'Government stamp' (p. 259) (see Contemporary Approaches, Feminist). This same system of social organisation can be seen to exclude and oppress Jude Fawley as a working-class man.

CHAPTER 2 **Arabella visits Jude seeking help. Sue dissuades him from offering assistance. Sue visits Arabella at her lodgings. She learns that Arabella is to marry her Australian 'husband', and announces that she is going to marry Jude**

Returning one evening from a public lecture on ancient history, Jude learns from Sue that Arabella has called to see him. As Jude prepares for bed, Arabella returns. She is unmarried and in trouble. Jude feels sympathetic and agrees to accompany Arabella to her lodgings. Sue fears that Arabella is attempting to entrap Jude again.

Jude returns to get his boots. He has not located Arabella outside in the street. Sue agrees to marry Jude, but with a sense of being conquered. Jude agrees not to pursue Arabella.

Next morning, Jude starts planning for the marriage. Sue now feels she was selfish on the previous night and determines to visit Arabella. She finds her still in bed. A chambermaid delivers a telegram announcing that Mr Cartlett, Arabella's Australian husband, has agreed to marry her lawfully. Sue proudly declares that she has agreed to marry Jude.

> When Jude returns for his boots, Sue declares 'O, I knew I could trust you! – how good you are!' (p. 265). She speaks with the confidence of hindsight; earlier she clearly experienced difficulty trusting Jude. Sue also uses the adjective 'good' to describe Phillotson's generosity towards her. This is not a world in which good and bad are absolute values. Sue's notion of goodness depends upon her **point of view**, and the perception that she has got her own way.
>
> Animal **imagery** recurs with Sue's wistful declaration, 'The little bird is caught at last!' Jude shows sensitivity to the implications of such entrapment with his reassuring response, 'No – only nested' (p. 268). At the start of the next chapter Sue perpetuates the sense of menace, describing legal marriage as 'a sort of trap to catch a man' (p. 271).

CHAPTER 3   **Jude and Sue postpone their marriage. They learn that Arabella has married Cartlett. They also learn that Arabella gave birth to Jude's son after her departure for Australia. Jude agrees to take responsibility for the boy's upbringing. The child arrives, and Sue feels that she and Jude should marry**

Jude and Sue are on the verge of having the banns read to initiate their marriage when Jude gives way to Sue's anxieties and agrees to postpone the proceedings.

Some weeks later, they receive from Arabella a letter and a South London newspaper. The newspaper reports Arabella's marriage to Mr Cartlett, the innkeeper. The letter reveals that Arabella gave birth to Jude's son, eight months after her departure for Australia. The boy has lived with Arabella's parents in Sydney, but they are sending him to her and she asks Jude if he will look after the child. Jude is shocked, but says that irrespective of his parentage the child deserves to be cared for. Sue concurs, and Jude sends a formal reply accepting responsibility for the boy's upbringing.

The next evening, around ten o'clock, Jude's son arrives at Aldbrickham. Nobody meets him at the railway station, and he finds his own way through the streets to Jude and Sue's lodgings. Soon after his arrival he calls Sue mother. She responds emotionally, suggesting to Jude that they should marry for the child's sake.

> Sue concurs passionately with Jude's weighty declaration that 'All the little ones of our times are collectively the children of us adults of the time, and entitled to our general care' (p. 274). This sense of one generation's benign nurturing of the next is quite contrary to Jude's own experience.

> There is, perhaps, a compromising self-centredness in Jude's proposal to educate the child for university: 'What I couldn't accomplish in my own person perhaps I can carry out through him?' (p. 278). He is projecting his own aspirations on to the boy, who proves an unsuitable vehicle for them. In Part Sixth, Chapter 1, Little Father Time asks if the university buildings are gaols. Jude tells him they are colleges in which he may one day study. The boy replies bluntly he would rather not (see p. 330).

> The narrator remarks that, 'Children begin with detail, and learn up to the general; they begin with the contiguous, and gradually comprehend the universal. The boy seemed to have begun with the generals of life, and never to have concerned himself with the particulars' (p. 278). This observation seems to highlight a peculiarity in Little Father Time's character, but a tendency to see life in terms of abstract generalities rather than concrete physical details is also evident in Jude and Sue. In the following chapter Sue regards their previous marriages not in terms of human relationships but in the quasi-scientific terms of 'the deterrent lesson we were taught by those experiments' (p. 283) (see Themes, on Ideal Forms & Material Reality).

Via Sacra avenue leading to the Forum in Rome
Octavia (d.11BC), sister of Emperor Augustus and wife of Marc Antony
Livia (58BC-AD29), wife of Emperor Augustus

Aspasia's eloquence (*c.*443BC) mistress of Pericles
Praxiteles (fourth century BC) Athenian sculptor
Phryne Athenian prostitute, who modelled for Praxiteles's statue of
Aphrodite
Let the day perish wherein I was born ... Job 3:3

CHAPTER 4   Jude and Sue make preparations for marriage, but at
the last minute they decide not to go through with the
ceremony

Jude's son, who has not been christened, has been known by the
nickname Little Father Time.

Sue and Jude make arrangements to marry. Before the actual
ceremony, Widow Edlin talks of the Fawleys' ill-luck with regard to
marriage. She tells of a man, thought to be one of their ancestors, who
was hanged on the brow of the hill near Brown House, at the point where
Jude first met Arabella. His wife had run away from him, their child died,
and she refused her husband access to the body. Trying to retrieve it, for
burial with his family, he was caught, found guilty of burglary, and sent
to the gibbet. His wife then went mad. Little Father Time interjects 'If I
was you, mother, I wouldn't marry father!' Sue dismisses it as a mere tale,
but the following day she is apprehensive, sensing that 'a tragic doom'
overhangs their family (p. 283).

A soldier and a young pregnant woman with a black eye are married
first. Then, another couple, the man just released from gaol. Sue hates the
vulgarity of the place and the people. Jude is eager to please her. They
grow indecisive. Walking and talking, they witness another wedding in
the parish church. After further deliberation they decide once again that
they should not marry, but agree that the child should not know of that
decision.

> The novel's portrayal of modern individuals debilitated by
> hypersensitivity and self-consciousness is elaborated here. Jude's
> suggestion that he and Sue are 'too thin-skinned – that they ought
> never to have been born' foreshadows his son's conviction that his
> own life is a mistake and his suicide (p. 286).

> Jude contends that it is because he and Sue are so 'horribly sensitive'
> that they find social conventions intolerable; they are 'folk in

whom domestic ties of a forced kind snuff out cordiality and spontaneousness' (p. 286). Sue suggests that this hypersensivity is set to become a general condition of human beings: 'Everybody is getting to feel as we do. We are a little beforehand, that's all' (p. 287). She predicts that future generations will refrain from reproduction on the basis that life has come to be seen as too painful to inflict upon the innocent unborn.

Melpomene Greek muse of Tragedy

the Jewish law-giver Deuteronomy 20:7

the Rubric regulations for conduct of services in *The Book of Common Prayer*

Atreus father of Agamemnon and Menelaus

Jeroboam 1 Kings 14:7, 9–10; Jeroboam was cursed by God for setting up idols of other deities

'Royal-tower'd Thame' from the poem 'At a Vatican Exercise in the College' (1628), by John Milton

a game o' dibs child's game, played with pebbles

CHAPTER 5   Jude, Sue and Little Father Time attend the Great Wessex Agricultural Show, watched by Arabella, who is also present

Packed trains converge on the town of Stoke-Barehills for the Great Wessex Agricultural Show. Arabella and her husband, Mr Cartlett, arrive from London at the same time that Jude, Sue and the child arrive from Aldbrickham.

Arabella infers that Jude and Sue are not married, as they are so engrossed with one another. The Cartletts follow separate courses around the Show. Arabella meets her old friend Anny. They watch Jude, and Arabella feels jealous. Then she meets Vilbert, the quack physician, who joins the women at an art exhibition, where all three watch Jude and Sue.

After buying a love-philtre from Vilbert, Arabella rejoins her husband who is drinking alcohol. Jude and Sue linger in the pavilion of flowers. Little Father Time shows no interest in any of the Show's attractions.

The art exhibition includes a model of Cardinal College, Christminster, made by Jude with Sue's assistance. In Part Fifth,

Chapter 7, Sue sells cakes at Kennetbridge fair, fashioned in pastry as 'reminiscences of the Christminster Colleges' (p. 312). These contrived **images** externalise Jude's obsession with the institution that has excluded him.

Words as well as images are deployed to create suggestive links across the text. So, 'the Government stamp', a phrase used by Sue to express her distaste for marriage, is used by the fraudulent Vilbert to guarantee the efficacy of his pills (p. 294). Sue's earnest use of the phrase contrasts with this deceitful use.

CHAPTER 6 **Jude and Sue pretend to be married, but are viewed with increasing hostility by their neighbours**

Jude and Sue are the subject of gossip. They pretend to be legally married. Jude has difficulty finding work, and suggests they move to an area where they are not known. Sue agrees as long as she is not separated from Little Father Time.

Jude first fulfils a commission to reletter the Ten Commandments written up in the local church. Sue assists him. Little Father Time arrives, crying because he has been taunted by school-fellows about his mother's character. Local women complain to the churchwarden that a disreputable couple have been hired to perform church work. Jude and Sue are asked to leave the job unfinished.

In Aldbrickham, Jude attends a committee meeting of the Artizans' Mutual Improvement Society. It is intimated that Jude's tarnished reputation has led to a decline in membership of the group. Jude auctions Drusilla's furniture. At the auction, the couple hear their private life being discussed by bidders.

Phillotson was subjected to the indignity of gossip after he allowed Sue to leave him. Now Jude and Sue, this obscure couple, are put under the intense scrutiny of public gaze. Respectable society appears a prohibiting milieu, that acts as a barrier to their happiness. Jude, like Phillotson, has to face a hostile committee. All three find that departure from orthodox ways of living disqualifies them from their customary profession.

The use of animal **imagery** to indicate entrapment and betrayal of trust recurs when Sue's pet pigeons are sold to a poulterer. Sue enables them to fly away, declaring with customary high seriousness: 'O why should Nature's law be mutual butchery!' (p. 308). Little Father Time's intense interest in this view of 'Nature's law' constitutes a further step towards his eventual acts of murder and his suicide. At points such as this Thomas Hardy's blatant contrivance is a clear departure from **realist** representation. He is distorting reality to create particular effects.

Pugin Augustus Pugin (1812–52), architect who inspired the Gothic Revival in England

Wren Christopher Wren (1632–1723), architect in the classical style, best known for St Paul's Cathedral in London; born near Shaftesbury

CHAPTER 7   Arabella, now a widow, meets Sue at Kennetbridge spring fair

For two and a half years, Jude and his family lead an itinerant existence, continually moving to find work. Nearly three years after the Agricultural Show, Arabella (now a widow) is at Kennetbridge spring fair with her friend Anny. She encounters Sue selling gingerbread and addresses her as Mrs Fawley. Sue has had two children and is pregnant again.

Jude has been unwell, after catching a chill doing stone-work on a music-hall. He makes cakes while confined indoors, and Sue sells them. Arabella has moved to Alfredston and claims to have found solace in religion since her husband's death. She has come to Kennetbridge to attend the placing by a popular London preacher of a foundation stone for a new chapel.

The 'obscure pair' have entered into 'a shifting, almost nomadic, life' (p. 309), which not only suits their peculiar circumstances, but also typifies that rootless wandering which is symptomatic of modern life (see Themes, on Modern Restlessness).

For some time it has been evident that Jude's beliefs have been changing; now 'he was mentally approaching the position which Sue had occupied when he first met her' (p. 310). Sue follows the opposite path, towards Jude's initial piety. This trend will be accelerated following the death of her children. Meanwhile,

Arabella gives an unconvincing display of piety following her husband's death. Here, Christian belief appears like a garment that can be put on or shed at will, according to circumstances or convenience (see Historical Background, on Loss of Faith).

CHAPTER 8   Arabella's desire for Jude has been reawakened

Arabella attends the placing of the foundation stone. Later, she tells her friend Anny that thoughts about Jude have displaced the Gospel from her mind. The women offer a lift on their horse and cart to an elderly man. It is Richard Phillotson, who has returned, as a last resort, to Marygreen, where the vicar is willing to employ him as a schoolmaster.

Phillotson does not remember Arabella, even though she was once one of his pupils, but the name of Jude Fawley supplies a connection between them. Arabella tells him that Jude is ill and Sue is troubled. She criticises Phillotson for allowing Sue to leave him.

Jude is discomposed when Sue tells of her meeting with Arabella, but he anticipates leaving the area soon. Sue is surprised that he wishes to return to Christminster. He says 'it is the centre of the universe to me, because of my early dream: and nothing can alter it' (p. 320). Three weeks later they return to that city.

Phillotson describes his return to Marygreen as 'a returning to zero, with all its humiliations'. His failure to realise his goals is evident to all who knew him before his departure for Christminster, laden with aspirations. He now sees the village as 'a refuge' (p. 317). The word suggests an animal escaping pursuers, rather than a human being fuelled by ambition for self-improvement. Jude, although equally a failure, refuses to surrender his ideal and heads for Christminster.

Contact with Sue seems to have coloured Phillotson's view of the world; there are echoes of her sentiments in his utterance: 'Cruelty is the law pervading all nature and society; and we can't get out of it if we would!' (p. 318). He has moved a long way from his initial injunction to Jude to show compassion for other creatures to this bleak pessimism.

A contented mind is a continual feast allusion to Proverbs 15:15: 'All the days of the afflicted are evil: but he that is of a merry heart hath a continual feast'

'Then shall the man be guiltless ...' Numbers 5:31: 'Then shall the man be guiltless from iniquity, and this woman shall bear her iniquity'

PART SIXTH: AT CHRISTMINSTER AGAIN

ESTHER (Apoc.) from the Book of Esther 14:2, describing Queen Esther's acceptance of humiliation in order to save the Jews

There are ... R. BROWNING from Robert Browning's poem 'Too Late'

CHAPTER 1   **Jude and his family arrive in Christminster and witness a procession of members of the university. Jude and Sue have to separate in order to take temporary lodgings**

Jude and his family arrive at Christminster on a day when a university prize-giving ceremony takes place. Jude explains the meaning of Latin inscriptions and the significance of carvings on the buildings to other members of the crowd, as they await the formal procession in the rain. He is recognised and taunted with his academic failure. He responds by discussing publicly the nature and causes of his failure, until silenced by a policeman.

The rain grows heavier as the procession passes. Sue notices Phillotson in the crowd. Lodgings are found for Sue and the children, but Jude has to go elsewhere. Sue admits to the landlady that she and Jude are not legally married; unhappy earlier marriages have deterred them from formalising their union. The landlady's husband insists they should have a single male lodger, so she tells Sue that she must leave the following day. Sue and Little Father Time spend that evening searching in vain for alternative lodgings.

Contrasts play an important role in this novel and the ceremonial procession heightens Jude's sense of his own failure; it passes 'across the field of Jude's vision like inaccessible planets across an object glass' (p. 328). Defiantly he insists 'it was my poverty and not my will that consented to be beaten' (p. 326). Jude recognises here that historical circumstances and prevailing social inequality have conspired against his best efforts to advance himself. The novel insists that individual lives are to a large extent contingent upon their social context (see Themes, on Individual Lives & Historical Periods).

Jude recognises that there is a particular character to the transitional time in which he lives that has shaped the nature of his experiences: 'I was, perhaps, after all, a paltry victim to the spirit of mental and social restlessness, that makes so many unhappy in these days!' He has followed Sue into rejection of orthodox guidelines for conduct, and finds himself 'in a chaos of principles – groping in the dark – acting by instinct and not after example'. His 'fixed opinions' have dropped away until his 'present rule of life' consists merely of 'following inclinations which do me and nobody else any harm, and actually give pleasure to those I love best' (p. 327) (see Themes, on Modern Restlessness).

A significant verbal echo occurs in this chapter. Jude says 'how good of you' to Sue for waiting patiently with him (p. 329). Sue has earlier used the word 'good' in similar fashion, not referring to any absolute standard, but when acknowledging the compliance of Jude or Phillotson with her wishes.

The blatant contrivance that characterises Thomas Hardy's narrative is evident in his location of Jude's lodgings in 'a narrow lane close to the back of a college, but having no communication with it' (p. 329). This sums up **symbolically** the entire course of Jude's adult life. The name, Mildew Lane, signifies the decay of Jude's aspirations. Equally contrived is Little Father Time's enquiry whether the great buildings are gaols, ironic as Jude has suffered exclusion from them, rather than incarceration.

At this point, Sue's allusions are biblical rather than classical, indicating that she is coming to espouse that piety which Jude under her influence has relinquished.

like the Lycaonians at Paul Acts 14:11, where the Lycaonians discern divine intervention when St. Paul heals a disabled person

> **from Caiaphas to Pilate** in New Testament accounts Jesus was taken from Caiaphas, the Jewish High Priest, to Pilate, the Roman procurator, and then to crucifixion

CHAPTER 2   Sue and Jude decide to lodge their family at the inn where Jude is staying. They go to collect the children, and discover that Little Father Time has hanged the other children and then himself. Sue gives birth prematurely to a still-born child

Sue talks with Little Father Time in their drab lodgings. He accuses her of cruelty because she is having another child while their current plight is sufficiently troublesome.

The following morning, Sue visits Jude at the inn where he has stayed. They decide to keep the family together in that inn, until something better can be arranged, and go to collect the children. While Jude is boiling eggs for the children's breakfast, Sue enters their room and discovers that Little Father Time has hanged the smaller children, and taken his own life in similar fashion. Sue faints. Jude is stunned by the horrific spectacle.

Jude summons the landlady, then runs to fetch a doctor. Sue is overcome by the guilty sense that her conversation with Little Father Time has driven him to act in this way. Jude says it was in the boy's nature. The doctor sees it as a sign of the times.

Spectators are drawn to the lodging-house by newspaper reports. The landlord is annoyed at this notoriety. The children are buried. Sue, still distraught, misses the funeral, but later in the day Jude finds her trying to stop a man filling the grave with earth. Jude takes Sue to her room and calls for the doctor. Late that evening Sue miscarries a still-born baby.

Contrasting **points of view** are registered at the start of this chapter. In Sue's eyes the College represents 'four centuries of gloom, bigotry, and decay'. She recognises, however, that Jude's perception of the institution is 'still haunted by his dream' and driven by 'a simple-minded man's ruling passion' (p. 332) (see Themes, on Relativism).

Sue impresses her view of the world upon Little Father Time, saying that 'all is trouble, adversity and suffering'. The boy, who is peculiarly receptive to this view responds by asking why adults conceive children, who don't ask to be born. He is horrified to learn that Sue is expecting another child, and accuses her of wilful cruelty. He declares, 'If we children was gone there'd be no trouble at all!' (p. 334) (see Historical Background, on Thomas Malthus).

Little Father Time says he should not have been born. He may appear constitutionally perverse in his gloomy outlook, but his father has expressed similar sentiments about his own life, and following the boy's suicide a doctor expresses the view that 'it is the beginning of the coming universal wish not to live' (p. 337). The stylised characterisation of Little Father Time indicates possible consequences of modern self-consciousness and hypersensitivity, at odds with the basic procreative instinct of human beings.

'We are made a spectacle unto the world, and to angels, and to men'
I Corinthians 4:9, referring to the persecution of the apostles
the eastward position controversy concerning whether Anglican priests should face the altar, with their backs to the congregation
Agamemnon tragedy by Aeschylus

CHAPTER 3   **Sue declares that she is still essentially Phillotson's wife. Arabella visits Jude and upsets Sue. Later, Jude finds Sue in a nearby church. Sue tells him they must part in order to remain friends**

Jude and Sue have taken new lodgings. He has returned to work; she is convalescing. Things have improved materially but both feel despondent, and their thoughts turn once again to legalising their marriage. But Sue, who has started attending services at the church of St Silas, is troubled that she has broken her marriage vows to Phillotson, and declares that she is still essentially the wife of her former husband.

Arabella, who has not replied to Jude's letter telling her of Little Father Time's death, arrives at their lodgings. Her mother has died and her father has returned from Australia. She now lives with him. Arabella refers to Sue as Jude's wife. Sue hurriedly repudiates that status, then leaves the room. Later, Jude finds Sue in the church, prostrated before a cross. She interprets the death of her children at the hands of Arabella's son as a sign that she has been wrong to live with Jude. After intense discussion they kiss, but Sue pushes Jude away, saying they must part in order to be friends as they were before they lived together.

Little Father Time has committed suicide. Sue now effectively destroys her former self by an act of determined 'self-renunciation' (p. 345). She was defiantly rebellious and unorthodox; now she wishes to sacrifice her past self on the altar of duty and conformity. Her pagan views are buried under Christian piety. Her love for Jude is subordinated to her status as wife to Richard Phillotson.

Little Father Time took his own life because his limited understanding persuaded him that life was intolerable. Jude and Sue become acutely aware of each other's restricted comprehension, and of the incompatibility that has arisen between their **points of view**. He refers to her 'extraordinary blindness'; Sue compares him to 'a totally deaf man observing people listening to music' (p. 351). In both cases, limited understanding is represented **figuratively**, as the lack of a sense organ.

my sensitive plant allusion to 'The Sensitive Plant' (1820), a poem by Percy Bysshe Shelley (1792–1822)

what sort of chiel is amangst them from 'On the Late Captain Grose's Peregrinations Through Scotland' (1789), a poem by Robert Burns (1756–96)

the pig that was washed turning back to his wallowing in the mire alludes to 2 Peter 2:22

let the veil of our temple be rent in two allusion to Mark 15:37–8, describing the crucifixion of Jesus Christ

CHAPTER 4   **Phillotson learns from Arabella that Sue has parted from Jude. He writes proposing remarriage and Sue agrees. Sue apprises Jude of this situation and suggests he should return to Arabella**

Richard Phillotson, watching the Christminster procession with his friend Gillingham, sees Sue with Jude. They discuss Sue on their return journey to Marygreen. Phillotson now regards her as innocent at the time of their divorce, and feels they should not have separated.

Y

Phillotson reads a newspaper account of the death of Jude's children. A few weeks later, he meets Arabella at Alfredston. She tells him that Jude and Sue no longer live together, and that Sue now considers herself Phillotson's wife. He envisages a rise in his fortunes following reunion with Sue. Gillingham cautions Phillotson against remarriage. Phillotson argues that her life with Jude and the children was the conclusion of her education. He writes to Sue suggesting that they might salvage something from their damaged lives.

On a foggy evening, a few days later, Sue arrives at Jude's door. As they walk towards the cemetery, she tells him she is returning to Phillotson. She advises Jude to take Arabella back. They part beside the grave of their children.

In one of the novel's characteristic reversals, Phillotson turns his vision once again to the future, with the possibility of renewing his life with Sue. It is brutally **ironic** that Phillotson considers her terrible experiences with Jude and the children to be a culmination to her education. Sue is excluded by social conventions of the day from pursuing an education appropriate to her intelligence and sensitivity.

Phillotson has never been an idealist in the sense that Sue and Jude are. He adapts his response to circumstances, without being bound to fixed principles. Such flexibility is a key to survival in this novel, although from Sue's idealistic **point of view** it is a diminution. She says to Jude: 'Every successful man is more or less a selfish man. The devoted fail ...' (p. 361).

'the world and its ways have a certain worth' from Robert Browning's poem 'The Statue and the Bust'

'Charity seeketh not her own' I Corinthians 13:5

CHAPTER 5   **Sue visits Phillotson in Marygreen. They marry for a second time**

Sue travels through the fog to Phillotson's house in Marygreen. She declares emotionally that her 'sin-begotten' children 'were sacrificed to teach me how to live! – their death was the first stage of my purification' (p. 363). He senses her physical aversion to him, which she nonetheless denies.

Phillotson has arranged their wedding for the following morning. After supper with Gillingham, Sue retires to her room at Widow Edlin's house. She destroys an embroidered nightgown, choosing instead to wear a coarse calico garment. Widow Edlin is bewildered. She tells Sue that she ought not to remarry as she is still in love with Jude. Sue is distraught.

Phillotson tells Gillingham that the marriage will help to restore his social standing which has deteriorated since he allowed Sue to leave him. Widow Edlin advises Phillotson against remarriage as Sue is still in love with Jude.

The marriage ceremony takes place in gloomy conditions. Phillotson reassures Sue that he will not make intimate demands on her, and her spirits lift a little.

A physical parallel to Jude and Sue's spiritual and emotional divergence occurs in this chapter. Sue departs for Marygreen, Jude's point of departure; Jude goes in the opposite direction to an unfamiliar spot, 'a dreary, strange, flat scene, where boughs dripped, and coughs and consumption lurked' (p. 362). This setting is an example of Thomas Hardy's use of landscape to mirror inner states, a technique which the critic John Ruskin (1819–1900) called **pathetic fallacy**.

steam-tram superseded the horse-tram in 1876

CHAPTER 6   **After confirming that Sue and Phillotson have remarried, Arabella directs her efforts towards securing remarriage to Jude**

On the day following Sue's remarriage to Phillotson, Arabella visits Jude's lodgings in the rain. She says her father has evicted her, so she is homeless and destitute, and she begs him to take her in. He arranges for her to lodge in a spare room.

On Sunday morning, Jude agrees that Arabella should go to Alfredston for news of Sue and Phillotson. She returns, confirming that the remarriage has taken place. Jude, in his wretchedness, wanders the city, ending up in a public house. Arabella heads for her father's pork-shop and demands his help towards her goal of remarrying Jude. She finds Jude in the inn. He drinks steadily. At length, Arabella guides him to her father's house, and helps him to bed.

Sue has observed that, 'Every successful man is more or less a selfish man' (p. 361). Arabella is sufficiently selfish to ensure the success of her contrivance to remarry Jude. It is a pragmatic response to circumstances rather than idealistic devotion that drives her. In one of the narrative's characteristic echoes, Arabella's return with Jude to her father's house recalls their 'entry into the cottage at Crescombe, such a long time before' (p. 376).

old Fuller's 'Holy State' Thomas Fuller's *The Holy State and the Profane State* (1642)

CHAPTER 7   **Arabella supplies Jude with alcohol. She and her father host a party. Jude, who is drunk, agrees before witnesses to remarry Arabella. The ceremony takes place**

Next morning, Arabella makes breakfast for her father, and tells him that she has 'a prize upstairs' (p. 377). She is confident that Jude will become her husband again.

Leaving Jude in bed, his illness exacerbated by heavy drinking, Arabella settles his account with his landlord, and arranges for his few possessions to be transported to Mr Donn's house. Arabella then supplies Jude with alcohol, while she secures a marriage licence, and arranges a party, ostensibly to promote her father's shop, but actually to entrap Jude.

The morning after the party, Tinker Taylor finds the revelry still in full swing. Arabella explains that she and Jude (who is clearly drunk) are to be married later that day. Jude's promises have been made before witnesses and his attempts to resist the ceremony are futile. The wedding takes place. On their return to the house Jude wants whisky. Arabella now gives him tea to sober him up.

Donn's shop, selling meat products, is a suitably corporeal setting for the death of Jude's aspirational ideals. He is plunged into a world of physical immediacy, where his own body enters a steady decline towards death.

her shorn Samson reference to Judges 16:19
Capharnaum place where Jesus seeks to live, and is rejected

the W—— of Babylon 'the Whore of Babylon', from Revelation
17:5. Puritans identified the Roman Catholic Church with this
figure

CHAPTER 8   Jude and Arabella live together in Christminster. As
his health deteriorates, Jude feels an intense need to see
Sue again. He travels to Marygreen and asks Sue to run
away with him. She refuses, and he returns to
Christminster

Jude and Arabella take lodgings near the centre of Christminster. His
health has grown precarious and he is unable to work. She feels the
burden of an invalid husband and accuses him of deception. As his health
deteriorates further, Jude asks Arabella to write to Sue. Arabella speaks
abusively of Sue. Jude threatens to kill her if ever she mentions Sue again.
Arabella then says she will send for Sue if she can be in the room during
the meeting. Jude agrees and is pacified, but Arabella does not send the
letter. Jude is tormented by Sue's failure to appear.

One day, Arabella returns home to find Jude missing, despite
driving rain outside. He has taken a train to Alfredston. Wrapped in his
great coat and a blanket he walks five miles to Marygreen, where he
instructs a boy leaving school to ask Mrs Phillotson to meet him in the
church. Sue says he is wrong to seek her out and that he was right to
marry Arabella again. Jude insists that Sue is his wife. Eventually, she
kisses Jude and tells him that her marriage to Phillotson has remained
unconsummated. She admits that she still loves Jude.

Jude argues that they both remarried when out of their senses; he
through drink, she through religion. He begs her to run away with him.
She refuses and goes to pray; Jude departs. She hears him cough as he
leaves and instinctively wants to help him, but instead she closes her ears.
In the wind and rain Jude passes the field where as a boy he had once
neglected to scare rooks. He inspects an inscription he made long before
on a milestone, now obscured by moss. He arrives in Christminster at ten
o'clock at night, drenched and weak.

Arabella, feeling the burden of having to care for an invalid
husband, accuses Jude of deception. This is **ironic**, as it was her acts
of deception that led to their marriage on both occasions.

The novel's **satirical** treatment of marriage is evident once again when Jude and Arabella's landlord suspects that they are not married when he sees them kiss; he is persuaded, however, when he hears them arguing, striking 'the note of ordinary wedlock' (p. 385). In Part Fifth, Chapter 5, the narrator refers to 'the antipathetic, recriminatory mood of the average husband and wife of Christendom' (p. 296). Just prior to this cynical evaluation, Arabella, observing Jude with Sue at the Great Wessex Agricultural Show, deduces that they are not married because they are so engrossed with one another (p. 297).

CHAPTER 9   **Sue enters into a physical relationship with Phillotson to punish herself for being in love with Jude**

Arabella meets Jude at the railway station. He declares that his reckless journey, in such poor health, was undertaken with the intention of ending his life.

At the same time, in Marygreen, Widow Edlin makes her customary late evening visit to help Sue with housework. Sue confides that Jude has been to Marygreen and she still loves him. She intends to do penance for this by going to bed with Phillotson.

In Phillotson's bedroom, Sue confesses to her husband that she has kissed Jude. He persuades her to swear on the New Testament that she will never see Jude again. She surrenders herself to him, despite her physical aversion. A storm rages outside.

Jude's desire to 'put an end to a feverish life which ought never to have begun' (p. 391) echoes Little Father Time's declaration that he should not have been born.

Although Jude's devotion to his intellectual heroes has been eroded by 'the grind of stern reality' (p. 392), he nonetheless sees, on his last walk past the Colleges, the spirits of those thinkers as he encountered them in his imagination on his first visit to Christminster. Arabella responds contrastingly, 'What do I care about folk dead and gone?' (p. 392). She is responsive to immediate physical circumstances, and has no interest in what is absent or abstract (see Themes, on Ideal Forms & Material Reality).

The raging storm is another instance of **pathetic fallacy,** mirroring Sue's inner turmoil.

Addison Joseph Addison, essayist (1672–1719)

Gibbon Edward Gibbon, historian (1737–94)

Johnson Samuel Johnson, writer and lexicographer (1709–84)

Browne Thomas Browne, prose writer (1605–82)

The Poet of Liberty Shelley

the great Dissector of Melancholy Robert Burton (1577–1640), author of *Anatomy of Melancholy* (1621)

Walter Raleigh poet, explorer and historian (*c*.1554–1618)

Wycliffe John Wycliffe, religious reformer (d.1384)

Harvey William Harvey, discoverer of the circulation of the blood (1578–1657)

Hooker Richard Hooker (1554–1600), bishop and author of *The Laws of Ecclesiastical Polity* (1593–7)

Arnold Matthew Arnold, poet and critic (1822–88)

Antigone tragedy by Sophocles

CHAPTER 10 **Widow Edlin tells Jude that Sue has entered into a physical relationship with Phillotson. Vilbert visits Jude and is dismissed. Vilbert drinks with Arabella and kisses her**

Jude recovers sufficiently to work again, but after Christmas his health breaks down once more. He and Arabella have moved still closer to the centre of Christminster. Jude's mind dwells on the failure of his early aspirations. Arabella offers to invite Sue to visit him, but Jude does not wish to see her again.

Widow Edlin pays Jude a visit and informs him that Sue, of her own free will, began sleeping with her husband after Jude's visit to Marygreen. Jude suggests that as a couple he and Sue were too advanced for their time.

Physician Vilbert arrives, at Arabella's request, but scurries away when Jude is scathingly critical of him. Vilbert meets Arabella. They drink and joke, and he kisses her.

Jude consoles himself with the belief that he and Sue together were too advanced for the time: 'Our ideas were fifty years too soon to be any good to us. And so the resistance they met with brought reaction in her, and recklessness and ruin on me!' (p. 400). This belief acknowledges that existing social conditions shape and constrain the course of individual lives. The university at Christminster is set to become less exclusive and to open its doors to intelligent men from the working class, but this will be too late for Jude, and for other worthy individuals who shared his fate and were condemned to live in obscurity, their potential unrealised (see Themes, on Individual Lives & Historical Periods).

CHAPTER 11   **Jude dies alone. Arabella postpones reporting his death so she can enjoy the Christminster festivities. Standing beside Jude's coffin, Arabella and Widow Edlin discuss Jude's life and Sue's unhappy situation**

It is summer. Jude is bedridden and emaciated. Sounds of festivity can be heard from the town. Arabella curls her hair before a mirror in the gloomy room, awaiting the arrival of her father. She grows impatient and leaves Jude alone in the house, in order to watch preparations for a concert and the guests arriving.

Jude, awakened by his cough, asks for water but finds he is alone. Returning home, Arabella discovers that Jude has died. Concealing this fact, she accompanies some of Jude's workmates to watch boat-racing. In the crowd by the river she meets Vilbert, who puts his arm around her waist and flirts with her.

Later, Arabella realises that if her husband is known to have died alone an inquest will be required. She tries to return home, but it is difficult to break free from the crowd. She forbids Vilbert to accompany her further, and enlists the services of a woman who makes funeral arrangements. By ten o'clock that night, Jude's corpse lies covered with a sheet.

Two days later, Arabella and Widow Edlin stand beside Jude's coffin. Noise from a ceremony conferring honorary degrees on the social elite is audible. The two women discuss Sue's unhappy life.

The acoustic environment plays an especially significant role in the later stages of this novel. Thomas Hardy creates an **ironic** counterpoint of telling contrasts. Jude dies alone, surrounded by the sound of the university's festivities. His dying words are interspersed grotesquely with hurrahs from the crowd outside; the sound of a waltz and applause as honorary degrees are conferred on the social elite is audible in the room where his corpse lies.

Arabella and Sue have been presented as diametrically opposed characters throughout the novel. In the closing scene, Thomas Hardy shows Arabella in dialogue with Widow Edlin, who tells her that Sue has become 'a staid, worn woman now', racked by the physical repulsion she feels for her husband (p. 408). Arabella self-centredly speculates that Jude might not find Sue attractive, as she is now. Yet for all the distance that exists physically and intellectually between the two women, Arabella displays some insight into the nature of Sue's love for Jude, which will not allow her to rest until she like Jude is dead. It suggests that there was common ground in Arabella and Sue's love for Jude, even if their manner of dealing with that emotion was radically different.

'Let the day perish ...' alludes to Job 3
boat-bumping race in which one boat bumps the stern of the one in front, and is rewarded by being placed ahead for the next race

PART THREE

CRITICAL APPROACHES

CHARACTERISATION

In a letter to the critic Edmund Gosse (1849–1928), Thomas Hardy observed of *Jude the Obscure* that 'the book is all contrasts'. Contrasts play an important role in characterisation (see Contemporary Approaches, Structuralist). Arabella Donn's sensual physicality contrasts with Sue Bridehead's chasteness and refined intelligence. When Jude meets Arabella, her coarseness stands in bold contrast to his unworldliness. Sue, on the other hand, appears almost ethereal when compared to Jude's outward appearance as a manual labourer.

Such contrasts give us a heightened sense of each character, although they run the risk of suggesting that Thomas Hardy is more concerned with types than individuals. Yet he does manage to convey personal idiosyncrasies as well as typical traits.

The attitudes of characters in *Jude the Obscure* are as liable to change as their material fortunes. Each has a distinct **point of view**, but changing circumstances alter the perceptions that follow from it. The novel depicts relative rather than absolute understanding, and characterisation displays far greater instability than is found in conventional **realist** fiction.

JUDE FAWLEY

At the start of the novel Jude Fawley is eleven years old. He has left the South Wessex village of Mellstock, following the death of his parents, and lives in Marygreen with his great-aunt Drusilla, who shows little interest in him. In contrast to her indifference, Jude is a caring, compassionate child, who cannot bear to hurt any living thing. He even displays sympathetic concern for earthworms in Part First, Chapter 2. As a young man he is described as 'a ridiculously affectionate fellow' (p. 85).

Jude is inspired by the example of his schoolmaster, Richard Phillotson, who departs for Christminster in the opening chapter, hoping one day to enter the university. All the events of the novel are seen in the light of that scholarly aspiration, which becomes the ruling passion of

Jude's own life. It is an idealistic vision that makes Jude increasingly an outsider to the life of the rural community.

Seven years later, Arabella Donn's friend Anny remarks that Jude has been 'very stuck up, and always reading' (p. 42), since his move to Alfredston, where he works as apprentice to a stonemason. He has taken this apprenticeship as a step towards his academic goal, a trade that can support him financially while he educates himself to the level required for admission to the university.

Anny also remarks that Jude is 'as simple as a child' (p. 42). The comparison recurs. For example, Jude is said to feel 'a childlike yearning' for Sue Bridehead (p. 122). He lacks worldly wisdom, and remains to the end incapable of the deviousness of some other characters in attaining their goals. He is duped early on by the quack doctor Vilbert, and is twice ensnared in marriage by Arabella's wiles. In contrast to the amoral practicality of these characters, two of the novel's survivors, Jude's idealism preserves his integrity and sense of honour in the face of the hardship and injustice he experiences.

Jude soon feels alienated. His vision of another kind of life separates him intellectually and emotionally from other working people, but the doors of academic life remain closed to him. His high principles are continually challenged by practical necessities, such as the demands of his married life with Arabella, which he recognises as 'a complete smashing up of my plans' (p. 57), yet Jude remains alert to ideals. He is appalled that the 'transitory instinct' of sexual attraction has caused him to forfeit the opportunity of 'showing himself superior to the lower animals, and of contributing his units of work to the general progress of his generation' (p. 62). He stays committed to grand goals rather than immediate gratifications.

At the beginning of Part Second, Jude is described as 'a young man with a forcible, meditative, and earnest rather than handsome cast of countenance'. He has a dark complexion, with dark eyes, a closely trimmed black beard and a 'great mass of black curly hair' (p. 77). Contrast is strongly registered through a **simile** appropriate to a stonemason when, towards the end of the novel, Jude's illness leaves him 'pale as a monumental figure in alabaster' (p. 387).

Jude's physical appearance is robust when he is healthy, but it regularly seems at odds with his inner condition. On his arrival in

Christminster, he is struck by 'the isolation of his own personality, as with a self-spectre, the sensation being that of one who walked, but could not make himself seen ,or heard' (p. 79). It is not difficult to see why Thomas Hardy applied the **epithet** 'the Obscure' to this man, struggling to render himself visible and audible in the world, yet destined to remain unknown beyond that small circle who know him in person. He wishes to join the ranks of his intellectual heroes, whose writings have lifted them from obscurity into widespread recognition by contemporaries and by posterity. Instead he remains an anonymous artisan, like the stonemasons who built the colleges, and the cathedrals of the Middle Ages.

Jude is drawn to his cousin Sue Bridehead as a kindred spirit. He is physically attracted to her, and is passionate to the point where his jealousy of Phillotson causes him to feel 'an unprincipled and fiendish wish to annihilate his rival at all cost' (p. 163). But he idealises her as he idealises Christminster. In Jude's view, 'his kiss of that aërial being had seemed the purest moment of his faultful life' (p. 216). He may be excluded from the company of Christminster scholars, but with Sue he feels a rare affinity: 'What counterparts they were!' (p. 144). That refined intimacy is noted by others, including Richard Phillotson and Arabella Donn, but it is not a relationship that can be sustained in the material world that the novel depicts.

Jude is initially pious in his Christian belief, but under Sue Bridehead's influence that belief wilts. Jude grows increasingly unorthodox in his view of all conventional social attitudes. **Ironically**, as he lapses from religious and social orthodoxy, Sue follows a path of self-denial that leads her back to Christian faith and to life as Richard Phillotson's obedient wife.

Jude feels that he is 'a social failure' (p. 129). Sometimes he attributes this to his own flaws and weaknesses, describing himself as 'a fellow gone to the bad' (p. 125). He identifies his two arch enemies as 'my weakness for women, and my impulse to strong liquor' (p. 353). When Sue deserts him, Jude is hesitantly prepared to blame his own selfishness: 'Perhaps – perhaps I spoilt one of the highest and purest loves that ever existed between man and woman!' (p. 354).

At other times, he believes that his failure has been decreed by some 'ruling Power', such as God, Fate, or Nature (p. 131). Or he recognises that his individual failings follow from specific historical circumstances: 'I was, perhaps, after all, a paltry victim to the spirit of mental and social restlessness, that makes so many unhappy in these days!' (p. 327). Sue casts that insight in explicitly political terms: 'You are one of the very men Christminster was intended for when the colleges were founded; a man with a passion for learning, but no money, or opportunities, or friends. But you were elbowed off the pavement by the millionaires' sons' (p. 151). Both Jude and Sue suffer as a consequence of their heightened self-consciousness and hypersensitivity, which Thomas Hardy identifies as an increasingly widespread characteristic of modern life.

RICHARD PHILLOTSON

Richard Phillotson is a village schoolmaster whose ambition is to gain a degree from the university at Christminster, and then to be ordained as a clergyman. At the start of the novel, Phillotson is in his early thirties, old enough to stand as a scholarly role-model in Jude's eyes, but still young enough to have aspirations of his own. Crucially, he is also young enough to be a credible rival for the love of Sue Bridehead, although Jude is appalled when she chooses to marry a man who is around twenty years older than he.

Phillotson wins Sue from Jude twice, but he remains a 'failure in the grand University scheme' (p. 101). When he first meets Sue, Phillotson is 'a spare and thoughtful person of five-and-forty, with a thin-lipped, somewhat refined mouth' (p. 102). He has a slight stoop, and wears a black frock coat, worn thin in patches. He is later said to have 'an unhealthy-looking, old-fashioned face, rendered more old-fashioned by his style of shaving' (p. 162). His hair is greying and curly. Overall, he has the look of a gentleman, 'dignified and thoughtful' (p. 174). He speaks rather slowly, and is described by his friend Gillingham as 'a sedate plodding fellow' (p. 230).

Sue recognises that Phillotson is 'a kind and considerate husband' (p. 174), in accordance with his courteous and compassionate conception of 'manliness or chivalry' (p. 231). He admires Sue's intellect, but in contrast to Jude's idealised estimation of her, Phillotson considers her his little friend.

Like Jude, he is self-consciously a man of integrity, who declares 'I have suffered for my acts and opinions, but I hold to them' (p. 317). In fact, Phillotson succumbs to Sue's influence to the point where he declares himself 'only a feeler, not a reasoner', and makes the radical observation that he cannot see why the family unit should not be woman and children without the man. He acknowledges 'I have out-Sued Sue in this'. In response to such departures from entrenched patriarchal values, his friend Gillingham argues that Sue 'ought to be smacked, and brought to her senses' (p. 232). Phillotson is too gentle to countenance such aggressive recrimination, but feminist critics would recognise here the inherent violence of patriarchy (see Contemporary Approaches, Feminist).

Far from showing integrity based in principle, Phillotson readily remarries Sue, despite his earlier feeling that it was cruel to remain her husband. Now he regards Gillingham as 'old-fashioned', in that his advice to resist Sue's renewed approaches fails to take account of modern Christminster views on the 'indissolubility of marriage', which have apparently taken hold in her mind. They are not views he shares, but, he concludes pragmatically, 'I shall make use of them to further mine' (p. 358).

There is **irony** in the claim to self-knowledge which rounds off this concerted attempt to justify his change of heart: 'Women are so strange in their influence, that they tempt you to misplaced kindness. However, I know myself better now' (p. 366). It is clear that he simply feels he has endured enough loneliness and misery and he will seize this opportunity to secure a compliant companion, even though he recognises that she is 'a luxury for a fogey like me' (p. 365).

ARABELLA DONN

The most striking thing about Arabella Donn is her physicality. The daughter of a pig-breeder, she is described as 'a complete and substantial female human', with dark eyes and voluptuous figure, compromised by 'coarseness of skin and fibre' (p. 39). Jude is drawn to her sensuality, yet repelled by her coarseness. That tells us a lot about his character: aspiring to intellectual and social refinement, yet driven also by sensual appetites and inclined to succumb to temptation.

Arabella inhabits the same restless modern world as Jude and Sue, but her response to it is very different. She too is mobile, moving from rural 'pig-jobbing' to bar-work in Christminster and in London; even emigrating to Australia. Crucially, Arabella has the capacity to adapt; she is a pragmatist, acting in response to immediate requirements and towards practical goals. This contrasts with the idealism of Jude and Sue, who invariably perceive large and weighty issues behind specific concerns. They extrapolate from the particular to the universal. Arabella is firmly embedded in the here and now. Early on, she regards Jude as 'a husband with a lot of earning power in him' as long as he can be persuaded to 'throw aside those stupid books for practical undertakings' (p. 58).

In Part First, Chapter 9, we are told that 'the world seemed funny' to Arabella and her friend Anny (p. 59). They regard life as a **comedy**; for Jude, on the other hand, life has the high seriousness of **tragedy**. This is Arabella's strength; it is also her limitation. She remains 'a woman of rank passions', with jealousy her most refined emotion (p. 378). She is portrayed as a calculating seductress, knowingly forming dimples which add to her attractiveness. She contrives to make Jude her husband on two occasions through exercise of her will and guile, and is ready to use blatant deception to gain her ends, whether it be telling lies or wearing false hair to make herself more alluring.

Jude feels that Arabella is 'not worth a great deal as a specimen of womankind' (p. 57). Yet he marries her twice, and that discloses how little control he is able to exercise over the course of his own life. In the interim she marries Cartlett, a publican. It is tempting to see a cruel **pun** in Arabella's family name: Jude's great desire is to be a don, a member of the university; instead he is ensnared twice, by a Donn. Arabella regards Jude's demise without sentimentality, as she has regarded the deaths of her mother, her husband Cartlett and her son. At the end of the novel she is concerned to make suitable provision for her own future requirements.

[handwritten margin note: Important reflection on Jude]

[handwritten note: — Important insight into her selfishness.]

SUE BRIDEHEAD

Sue Bridehead's 'vivacious dark eyes and hair' signal familial resemblance to her cousin Jude who is similarly dark (p. 102). She is 'light and slight, of the type dubbed elegant'. In contrast to Arabella Donn, Jude's other lover, 'there was nothing statuesque in her; all was nervous motion' (p. 90). She embodies that restless mobility which is indicative of modernity in this novel. Her old-fashioned great-aunt Drusilla alludes disparagingly to Sue's 'tight-strained nerves' (p. 110).

Like Arabella, Sue deserts then returns to her first husband. They both love Jude. But Thomas Hardy conceived these two women as dramatically contrasting characters. Arabella is physically robust and sensual; Sue is delicate to the point of seeming ethereal, and she abhors physical contact. Arabella's knowledge is purely of a practical kind, derived from the hurly-burly of experience; Sue's intellect is directed to ideals and abstractions, detached from the world of human interaction.

Sue is described as 'an epicure in emotions', suggesting an indulgence in feelings. She refers to her own 'curiosity to hunt up a new sensation' (p. 173). In fact, Sue has channelled all her emotions into ideas, to the detriment of her intellectual powers and her feelings. Her intellectuality is emotional rather than rational, and that proves a weakness. She sees herself as 'a woman tossed about, all alone, with aberrant passions, and unaccountable antipathies' (p. 205). She finds it difficult to act upon her insights, to pursue her convictions to practical conclusions. Sue is too sensitive, too self-conscious to achieve results. This contrasts with Arabella, who lacks vision beyond her immediate needs and is clever in purely practical terms, but does manage to influence events and shape circumstances that directly concern her.

Jude perceives Sue as his counterpart, an ideal kindred spirit. The narrator observes that as they talked 'there was ever a second silent conversation passing between their emotions, so perfect was the reciprocity between them' (p. 203). But there is a more palpable sense in which they are counterparts. Sue suffers from the exclusion of women from university education during the Victorian period, and consequently squanders her considerable intellectual resources. The training-school for teachers she attends does not come close to matching the horizons opened by her own reading. Her conversation reflects her interest in the writings of advanced thinkers such as Auguste Comte (1798–1857) and John Stuart Mill (1806–73). It is not only Jude who falls victim to exclusion based in prejudice.

Jude is initially attracted by a photograph of Sue. Phillotson, as her husband, comes to own a copy of the same photograph. Both men are devoted to this image as to a religious icon. Their intense attachment contrasts starkly with Arabella's unsentimental disregard for the photograph given to her by Jude, which he finds in a broker's shop, after she has gone to Australia.

Even when they are physically together, Jude continues to regard Sue as 'more or less an ideal character', cloaking her in 'curious and fantastic day-dreams' (p. 89). He views her as 'a woman-poet, a woman-seer, a woman whose soul shone like a diamond' (p. 350). Late in the novel, he is still able to view her as his 'guardian-angel' (p. 353) rather than a flesh-and-blood woman.

Sue has lived in London, and Jude is initially drawn to her apparent metropolitan refinement, remote from his own rustic upbringing. Observing her in Christminster, 'He could perceive that though she was a country-girl at bottom, a latter girlhood of some years in London, and a womanhood here, had taken all rawness out of her' (p. 90). Importantly, the rural element in her constitution is still discernible. Sue is a transitional figure, neither country-girl nor urban sophisticate, but an uneasy amalgam of the two, self-aware and prone to 'super-sensitiveness' (p. 278). Significantly, she ends up in Marygreen, unhappily married to a village schoolmaster.

Sue has three relationships with men: with a Christminster undergraduate, who dies young; with Richard Phillotson, an older man; and with Jude, four years younger than her. Jude describes her as 'absolutely the most ethereal, least sensual woman I ever knew to exist without inhuman sexlessness' (p. 344). Yet although men find her sexually attractive, in each relationship she shies from sexual contact. Even though she has children with Jude, it is clear that Sue finds sexual intercourse distasteful and avoids it as far as circumstances permit. A 'wild look of aversion' crosses her face when she eventually surrenders herself to Richard Phillotson, her husband (p. 398).

The anxiety that underlies her chasteness produces psychologically complex characterisation, and Thomas Hardy portrays Sue's personality as fraught with tensions, vacillations and contradictions. Her 'common trick' of 'putting on flippancy to hide real feeling' makes interpretation more difficult for those who seek to know her (p. 151). Jude, who initially tries to persuade himself that he will be content with knowing Sue as 'a kindly star' and 'an elevating power' (p. 91), is eventually driven by frustration to criticise her as 'a phantasmal, bodiless creature' lacking 'animal passion' (p. 260) and 'incapable of real love' (p. 240). He says that she is 'upon the whole, cold, – a sort of fay, or sprite – not a woman!' (p. 353). Phillotson finds her 'puzzling and peculiar' (p. 230), a 'maddening compound of sympathy and averseness' (p. 251).

Initially, Sue is seen to be a sceptic, attending church services, but unable to espouse orthodox Christian belief. She declares herself an atheist, and is attracted to the religion and philosophy of ancient Greece. More generally she rebels against received opinion and social convention, expressing views which may be regarded as feminist in their hostility towards the assumptions underlying patriarchal society. She regards marriage as 'a sordid contract, based on material convenience in householding, rating, and taxing, and the inheritance of land and money by children' (p. 209). Sue recognises that Jude is a victim of social injustice arising from the class-based nature of English society; as a working-class man he is subjected to indignities and disadvantages which would not be experienced by the wealthy. Beneath such analytical insights lies a rebellious nature which, as aunt Drusilla's nurse recalls, was manifested as impertinence when Sue was a child.

[Following the death of her children, Sue enters a phase of self-denial. Her previous, rebellious self is effectively destroyed, and she acquiesces to orthodoxy in religious belief and social practice. This is not altogether inconsistent with her earlier behaviour: 'There was no limit to the strange and unnecessary penances which Sue would meekly undertake when in a contrite mood' (p. 268). It is appropriate that the final words of the novel, spoken by Arabella as she stands beside Jude's corpse, refer to Sue, Jude's counterpart who has consented to be buried alive in obscure Marygreen.] – *How she reacts to the society she lives in suppressing her to the point that*

L<small>ITTLE FATHER TIME</small>

The son of Jude and Arabella is also called Jude Fawley, but he is generally known as Little Father Time because he is 'a boy with an octogenarian face' (p. 311). Jude, as a child, is said to be 'an ancient man in some phases of thought, much younger than his years in others' (p. 26), but his son has inherited only the former quality. He is 'Age masquerading as Juvenility' (p. 276), with an old man's weary spirit in his young body. He walks with 'a steady mechanical creep' that conveys 'an impersonal quality' (p. 277). He is small, pale with large eyes, and a fixed expression of fear. His face resembles a tragic mask, and he believes that 'rightly looked at there is no laughable thing under the sun' (p. 276). He cannot see flowers without thinking of them withered within days.

Jude is driven by the hope that he can elevate his standing, intellectually and socially; but his son is 'singularly deficient in all the usual hopes of childhood' (pp. 288–9). Both Jude and Sue are drawn to the realm of ideas and abstractions. Little Father Time is still more detached from physical reality; he is 'in the habit of sitting silent, his quaint and weird face set, and his eyes resting on things they did not see in the substantial world' (p. 280).

Arabella, in the process of seducing Jude declares, 'I suppose it is natural for a woman to want to bring live things into the world' (p. 55). But Little Father Time says 'I ought not to have been born' (p. 332), a sentiment his father has uttered but never acted upon. The boy, however, kills Sue's children and takes his own life, following her announcement to him that she is expecting another child. This horrifies him, as he has witnessed the difficulty Jude and Sue experience in providing for their children. The act can be seen as a perverse application of the ideas of Thomas Malthus (1766–1834) (see Historical Background, on Thomas Malthus).

MINOR CHARACTERS

AUNT DRUSILLA
Jude's great-aunt Drusilla raises him following the death of his parents, but she expresses the wish that he too had died, rather than living to trouble her. Her primary role in the novel is to insist that members of the Fawley family are not suited for marriage or, by implication, for procreation. The jaded old woman's sour anti-life sentiments are translated into action by Little Father Time.

WIDOW EDLIN
Although Widow Edlin is a more benign figure than Drusilla, she also warns that their family history does not bode well for Jude and Sue. Nonetheless, she wishes them well, and is unable to comprehend the

intense self-consciousness that proves an insurmountable obstacle, preventing their marriage. She remarks that when she was young people were more easy-going, and happier as a consequence.

VILBERT

Vilbert is an itinerant quack doctor, a medical charlatan who cynically takes advantage of the gullibility of the uneducated rural poor. At a time when the practice of medicine in England was becoming increasingly professionalised, Vilbert appears to be a vestige of former times, but his knowledge of folk medicines is not authentic.

He dupes Jude, when a boy, by promising to bring him books in return for new customers. Jude fulfils his part of the bargain, but Vilbert characteristically does not reciprocate. He is self-serving, but he is a survivor. In this he resembles Arabella, and it is fitting that as Jude lies dying Vilbert and Arabella are together, enjoying the Christminster festivities. Arabella even considers marriage to this duplicitous man as a way of making suitable provision for her future.

GILLINGHAM

Gillingham, a schoolmaster, is an old friend of Richard Phillotson. By introducing him into the narrative, Thomas Hardy is able to externalise, through conversations and correspondence, the debate occurring in Phillotson's mind concerning the rights and wrongs of his relationship with Sue. The renewed friendship also emphasises through contrast the isolation of Jude Fawley towards the end of his life. Jude has no such friend in whom to confide.

THEMES

MODERN RESTLESSNESS

Aunt Drusilla views Christminster as an alien world and refuses to take seriously young Jude's suggestion that he might visit Phillotson there, even though it is only about twenty miles away. During the second half of the nineteenth century, technological innovations such as the railway network and the electric telegraph had a dramatic effect upon spatial relationships, and increasingly upon social relationships within England. In *Jude the Obscure* Thomas Hardy depicts a society becoming accustomed to the possibilities of greater mobility offered by such developments. Marygreen has been Drusilla's world, but Arabella Donn, a countrywoman of a younger generation, displays no anxiety at the prospect of moving to London. She even emigrates to Australia, on the other side of the globe.

These developments had a psychological as well as a physical impact, contributing to the perception that individuals need not follow their ancestors in feeling bound to a particular location or a way of life. Horizons were expanding in more ways than one. Jude's aspirations arise from this sense that he can move from the 'small sleepy place' where he grew up (p. 11), into another social sphere and the intellectual world of the university. But social mobility proves far less straightforward than bodily travel. Jude walks physically amongst the scholars of Christminster, yet, in an **ironic** evocation of Arabella's departure, 'he was as far from them as if he had been at the antipodes' (p. 96). Heightened expectations are not matched in reality. Jude remains, in effect, closer to Arabella than to the dons.

Older characters are bemused by modern attitudes to marriage. Part of modern restlessness, as it is delineated in *Jude the Obscure*, is distrust of received social conventions. Sue and Jude no longer feel at home in attitudes formed in the past. They have become displaced from traditional assumptions, but have not managed to establish new codes of conduct. Instead they act by instinct, and consequently they often appear anxious and agitated.

Not only has the old church at Marygreen been replaced by a new one, but, Sue affirms, the cathedral in Christminster has been superseded in importance by the railway station. This can be read literally: the architect of the village's new church building has 'run down from London and back in a day' (p. 13). Isolated hamlets such as Marygreen have become readily accessible to the influence of city-dwellers. It can also be read **figuratively**: old stable truths have given way to more provisional forms of comprehension. Greater mobility brings relative rather than absolute understanding as **points of view** change.

INDIVIDUAL LIVES & HISTORICAL PERIODS

A crucial insight offered by *Jude the Obscure* is that the historical period in which one lives shapes expectations and curtails options in important ways. It is ironic that by the end of the novel ambitious young men with backgrounds comparable to Jude's own are said to be gaining access to the university. If Jude had been born a few decades later he might have realised his cherished goal. More generally, Jude feels: 'I was, perhaps, after all, a paltry victim to the spirit of mental and social restlessness, that makes so many unhappy in these days!' (p. 327). Historical forces do not entirely determine the course taken by individual lives, but they do have an inescapable effect.

Jude and Sue, in their partial understanding of the world around them, have recourse to concepts such as Fate, Necessity, Nature's Law, and Nemesis when discussing that 'something external to us which says, "You shan't!" ' (p. 337). In fact, that 'something external' can usually be identified as the structure of the historical moment in which they live.

Sue's radical views on marriage and religion appear far less controversial at the start of the twenty-first century than they did at the end of the nineteenth century. Her attitudes would not seem especially unusual now, and the inner crisis she experiences could be avoided. Sue presciently envisages the astonishment of future generations looking back at 'the barbarous customs and superstitions of the times that we have the unhappiness to live in' (p. 215). In the given historical context of her day, she becomes hypersensitive and intensely self-conscious. She is afflicted by 'a creeping paralysis' arising from 'an awe, or terror, of conventions I don't believe in' (p. 329). She craves the freedom she felt as an unselfconscious infant, but Jude recognises that she is 'a product of civilization' (p. 139), even as she reacts against received opinion.

The narrative of *Jude the Obscure* makes considerable use of contrasts between ancient and modern life and beliefs, ranging from the changing face of Marygreen, where a well-shaft is 'probably the only relic of the local history that remained absolutely unchanged' (p. 12), to Sue's intellectual love for ancient Greek philosophical idealism. One of the functions of such contrasts is to highlight changing **points of view** throughout history. Social conventions accepted in one time or place seem inappropriate or unacceptable elsewhere.

Jude comes to regard Sue as 'one of the women of some grand old civilization' rather than 'a denizen of a mere Christian country' (p. 271). Sue, perceiving the shortcomings of prevailing social conventions, is free to reject them, but she must live with the consequences that inevitably follow from that choice. She and Jude are able to inhabit a 'dreamy paradise' for a while (p. 272), but they soon fall back with a jolt into the historical world.

IDEAL FORMS & MATERIAL REALITY

In a society experiencing rapid change, unchanging ideal forms seem to offer a stable and comprehensible alternative to the chaotic events of the material world. It was during a turbulent period of history, that the Greek philosopher Plato (c.429–347BC) conceived his influential model of an ideal reality existing beyond the reach of human senses and beyond the illusory world of material things.

Sue Bridehead is drawn to such an ideal reality, and seems more at ease with abstract conceptions than with physical existence. Jude too is driven by ideas, rather than settling for a life of manual labour and relative material security. But the novel shows that 'high thinkings' often run counter to 'immediate needs' (p. 83). Idealism can prove debilitating.

Thomas Hardy seems to be indicating a trend in modern life away from specifics towards ideals, making practical living increasingly difficult. The problems that Jude and Sue face are largely a consequence of their failure to respond pragmatically to material situations. Sue responds to the boy's tears by saying to Jude 'There's more for us to think about in that one little hungry heart than in all the stars of the sky ...' (p. 279). But she is unable to sustain that focus upon immediate necessities. Little Father Time, still more blind to particulars, proves incapable of coping with life's challenges.

Arabella Donn, a sensual woman, has no time for the ideal; she is focused squarely on physical reality, untroubled by ideas or principles. Vilbert, the quack physician, is similarly focused, and both characters are survivors. It might be concluded that Thomas Hardy is advocating this unintellectual, eminently pragmatic way of living. But there are evident limitations to it. Arabella's lack of emotion at the deaths of her son and her husbands is indicative of her narrow self-centredness.

RELATIVISM

Orthodox Christianity proclaims God's absolute knowledge. In *Jude the Obscure* there is no evidence to suggest the existence of the Christian God; rather there is **ironic** reference to 'the flaw in the terrestrial scheme, by which what was good for God's birds was bad for God's gardener' (p. 16). All values are relative, and when characters achieve a degree of understanding it is provisional and governed by their **point of view**. The narratorial voice, although ostensibly resembling the **omniscient narrator** of conventional **realist** fiction, can shed only limited light upon events and motives (see Narrative Structure & Technique).

As well as being a technical issue, relativity of perception and comprehension assumes thematic importance throughout the novel. So, Sue in her pagan phase tells the Christian Jude, 'you don't know how bad I am, from your point of view' (p. 135). Later, on the verge of abandoning him, Sue tells Jude that although she remains his wife from his point of view, she is returning to Phillotson whose wife she now considers herself to be (see p. 346). Jude might have predicted this change from her earlier relativistic declaration that 'it is as culpable to bind yourself to love always as to believe a creed always, and as silly as to vow always to like a particular food or drink!' (p. 223).

At its simplest, this relativity of perception and comprehension is expressed by Sue's platitude, 'Things seem so different in the cold light of day' (p. 154). Not only do different people interpret events in different ways, but their mode of interpretation is itself liable to change according to alterations in their circumstances.

LANGUAGE & STYLE

Jude the Obscure is a novel of contrasts. This extends to Thomas Hardy's use of language. The narrator's voice is educated and resourceful, with a measured taste for polysyllabic vocabulary. It is a voice which uses words such as 'chimerical', 'supercilious', 'deprecatingly', and 'soliloquizing', but which does not obtrude in a way which suggests great distance from the characters. Sue and Jude, of course, through their efforts at self-education, are perfectly capable of using such words themselves.

But there are characters in the novel who speak a distinctive Wessex **dialect**, employing local vocabulary and nonstandard grammatical construction. Aunt Drusilla's speech, for example, is created by Thomas Hardy to evoke a life led in an isolated rural community. The shepherd who gives shelter to Jude and Sue in Part Third, Chapter 2, displays the narrow geographical limits of his experience in his manner of speaking: 'You can bide here, you know, over the night – can't 'em mother? The place is welcome to ye. 'Tis hard lying, rather, but volk may do worse' (p. 138). Such dialect speech registers the world from which Jude seeks to move towards the sophisticated discourse of Christminster.

In *Tess of the d'Urbervilles* (1891), Phase the First, Chapter 3, Thomas Hardy remarks that Tess 'spoke two languages: the dialect at home, more or less; ordinary English abroad and to persons of quality'. The distinction indicates that class, as well as locality and education, influences manner of speech. Hardy draws attention to the difference between the way Tess speaks and her mother's dialect. It is not just a difference of expression, but of the ways in which they comprehend the world. The rate of change in nineteenth-century England was such that when mother and daughter were together 'the Jacobean and Victorian ages' were juxtaposed, and 'a gap of two hundred years as ordinarily understood' was closed. The crucial distinction is that Tess has been educated by a London-trained teacher.

Phillotson and Gillingham are trained teachers, who can talk of Plato and Shelley, yet they still employ dialect words. They live in a transitional phase of history, bridging traditional and modern ways of life. In Part Fourth, Chapter 4 the words 'lumpering', 'toled', and 'good-now' signal that the education these two men have received has not drawn them totally into the system of standard English.

Thomas Hardy uses quotations from literature and philosophy to show the more formal and self-conscious uses of language which have fired Jude's imagination and fuelled his aspirations. These are voices polished for print, sophisticated and refined, and remote from the dialect spoken by the folk of Marygreen. Jude has entered that eloquent world mentally, but remains excluded from it physically.

Jude the Obscure contains many allusions to the Bible. These introduce another kind of language, bearing the weight of traditional forms of religious belief. The authority of the Bible was being challenged by influential figures amongst Thomas Hardy's contemporaries, but in this novel, which offers no consoling picture of a caring God, biblical references are seen to have continuing relevance to the practical conduct of modern lives, especially to problems that arise in relationships between men and women. In a novel that addresses the rival claims of spiritual and material views of reality, this use of the Bible appears firmly grounded in the material world.

NARRATIVE STRUCTURE & TECHNIQUE

STRUCTURE

Jude the Obscure is divided into six parts, each headed with a title that indicates the location of its action. This is appropriate to a novel that addresses restlessness as a symptom of modern life. Each part is divided into chapters and is prefaced by an **epigraph**. This epigraph is a quotation which highlights certain thematic concerns central to that section. So, Part First starts with a quote from an apocryphal book of the Bible on the power that women may exercise over men, and then proceeds to show Arabella Donn captivating Jude Fawley.

NARRATION

In the closing pages of *Jude the Obscure* the narrator, speaking as 'the chronicler of these lives', makes a direct request for 'the reader's attention' (p. 401). The term 'chronicler' suggests that narration involves a straightforward record of events, but although what happens in the novel can be summarised without too much difficulty, interpretation of those events is far from straightforward.

This is partly because **point of view** plays an important role in the novel. For example, Jude as a boy regards Phillotson as a role model to follow, but later he regards the same man as a rival for the love of Sue Bridehead, and then as an unworthy husband for her. Sue herself is regarded idealistically by Jude as a kind of divine creature. At the same time, Phillotson sees her patronisingly as a little girl, requiring his protection. Aunt Drusilla adds a third point of view, recalling with disapproval Sue's behaviour when a child. None of these angles corresponds to Sue's own view of herself, which is itself changeable.

The 'chronicler' has characteristics of a conventional **omniscient narrator**, with God-like knowledge of all that occurs, and access to the workings of each character's mind. Thoughts and feelings are duly reported, but all the characters in *Jude the Obscure* have only partial understanding of the world around them and of their own responses to it. Little Father Time's grotesque acts of murder and suicide form the most dramatic instance of a character acting with a limited or flawed grasp of a situation, but all through the novel other characters are similarly blinkered.

A conventional omniscient narrator can be relied upon to shed light on hidden motives and to offer explanation for unexpected consequences. The narrator of *Jude the Obscure* preserves an air of mysterious forces at work, especially with regard to Sue Bridehead (see Contemporary Approaches, Psychological). The narrator's comments tend to add to the novel's gloomy atmosphere, or to heighten the sense of portentousness that characterises Jude and Sue's insistently serious dialogue. Indeed, the narration often implies their points of view without explicitly attributing sentiments to them.

A good illustration of this is the comment which follows the discovery of Little Father Time's corpse. The boy's face is said to express the lamentable history of his father's life with Arabella and with Sue: 'He was their nodal point, their focus, their expression in a single term. For the rashness of those parents he had groaned, for their ill-assortment he had quaked, and for the misfortunes of these he had died' (p. 337). This does not clarify the situation, but adopts the tense, heightened tone of Jude and Sue's pronouncements to convey a sense that individual human lives are tyrannised by the legacy of past actions. This narratorial observation occurs while Sue is viewing the bodies of the children. It is not attributed to her, but we may assume that the narrator is at this moment closely aligned with Sue's perception of events.

PATTERNING

There is evident tension in Thomas Hardy's later fiction between his careful attention to details which grant a sense of faithfulness to reality and blatant contrivance which separates his writing from conventional literary **realism**. In *Jude the Obscure*, narrative events are patterned in a way that is almost geometrical. So, Jude moves through the course of the novel from Marygreen to the heart of Christminster; Sue starts in Christminster and ends in Marygreen. Arabella leaves Jude and then returns to him; Sue leaves Phillotson and then returns to him. Sue shifts from scepticism to conviction; Jude follows the opposite path from belief to lack of belief.

These lines seem clear when abstracted from events, but the events themselves are far less well defined, entangled in obscure motives and conflicting perceptions. This is an appropriate tension in a novel extensively concerned with relationships arising between ideas and actualities (see Themes, on Ideal Forms & Material Reality). Ideal forms seem to promote understanding; material reality frustrates it. Can ideas serve as a reliable guide to living in the physical world? Is the physical world without ideas merely a chaotic site of the scramble to survive?

IRONY

Irony arises when one thing is said, but another is understood, or when the significance of an event can be read in terms that are at odds with its apparent meaning. In *Jude the Obscure*, perception is relative to situation and understanding alters as **point of view** changes, so there is ample scope for irony. For example, in the closing pages of the novel, joyful, celebratory noises from the Christminster festivities are juxtaposed with Jude's dying moments. The fading away of this life of failure passes ironic commentary upon those sounds of vitality and success.

ANIMAL IMAGERY

A pattern of animal **imagery** emerges in the novel. These images present animals as victims, trapped or hunted, and incapable of comprehending fully the nature of their plight. They contribute to the novel's gloomy mood, and more specifically suggest parallels with the lives of characters, especially Jude and Sue.

The parallels can be explicit. A **simile** compares Jude to 'a pet lamb' (p. 53). Arabella is said to make a 'tigerish indrawing of breath' (p. 54).

She speaks of Sue as 'the rat that forsook the sinking ship' (p. 385). Near the start of the book Jude, with great reluctance, slaughters a pig. In Part Sixth, Chapter 8 he says to Arabella: 'I feel now that the greatest mercy that could be vouchsafed to me would be that something should serve me as I served that animal!' (p. 384). It is part of Jude's early aspiration to show himself 'superior to the lower animals' (p. 62). The novel appears to indicate that despite the sophistication of scholarship, human life retains much in common with the instinctive and precarious life of other creatures.

Satire

It is not at all times clear how we should respond to *Jude the Obscure*. Events which seem **tragic** from one **point of view** seem **farcical** from another. Little Father Time's acts of murder and suicide suggest tragedy, yet he is such a contrived figure, such a calculated grotesque, that he seems more a stylised **caricature** than a credible character.

There are overt references in the novel to **satire**, a mode of literature that exposes and mocks human folly and vice, and tends to produce exaggerated or distorted figures like Little Father Time. Phillotson speaks of Sue 'with good-humoured satire' (p. 107); when Jude receives Sue's letter announcing her engagement to Phillotson, 'Everything seemed turning to satire' (p. 169); and faced with Jude's sarcasm following her reversion to Christian belief, Sue declares, 'Don't satirize me: it cuts like a knife!' (p. 351).

The novel is openly satirical in its treatment of marriage. A landlord suspects that Jude and Arabella are not married when he sees them kiss; he is persuaded, however, when he hears them arguing, striking 'the note of ordinary wedlock' (p. 385). In Part Fifth, Chapter 5, the narrator refers to 'the antipathetic, recriminatory mood of the average husband and wife of Christendom' (p. 296). Just prior to this cynical evaluation Arabella, observing Jude with Sue at the Great Wessex Agricultural Show, suspects that they are not married because they are so engrossed in one another.

ENVIRONMENT

Environment plays a significant role in Thomas Hardy's fiction. Topographic features, such as Egdon Heath in *The Return of the Native* (1878) or Stonehenge in *Tess of the d'Urbervilles* (1891) add to the atmosphere and enhance the production of meaning. *Jude the Obscure* is unusual amongst his novels in that much of the action occurs in a city, but Thomas Hardy still makes environment an active component of his text.

Recurrent features in the landscape help to configure meaning, notably the spot where a gibbet once stood, near the Brown House barn. It was the spot where Jude's parents separated, and early on it becomes the focal point of 'the upland whereon had been experienced the chief emotions of his life' (p. 73). Repeated references to this place suggest some impersonal force at work, patterning events and determining the lives of individuals who believe they are acting freely. Jude chooses an equally inauspicious location in Christminster when he arranges to meet Sue where a cross in the pavement marks the site of martyrdom (see p. 99). Jude is following country custom in arranging the assignation out of doors. Even in making the choice he is not acting freely.

Jude believes that reading brings enlightenment, and he applies that belief to the world around him, attempting to decipher Christminster as he would read a book. The college buildings are dense with meaning for him, but in the later stages of the novel, they are swathed in thick fog, suggesting the limits to Jude's comprehension of this world. The acoustic environment also plays an important role, especially when Jude, in bed during his final illness, hears the sounds of celebration from the university festivities beyond the walls of his room. Thomas Hardy makes extensive use of such **ironic** juxtaposition.

The novel's environment can appear blatantly contrived. Jude finds lodgings in 'a narrow lane close to the back of a college, but having no communication with it' (p. 329), a location which seems to **symbolise** the entire course of Jude's adult life. In order to heighten the effect Thomas Hardy calls it Mildew Lane, the name signifying the decay of Jude's dreams and aspirations. Such artifice would seem glaringly inappropriate in a conventionally **realist** novel, but it can be accommodated within Hardy's highly stylised text.

PART FOUR

TEXTUAL ANALYSIS

TEXT 1 (from PART SECOND, CHAPTER 2, PAGES 83–5)

Necessary meditations on the actual, including the mean bread-and-cheese question, dissipated the phantasmal for a while, and compelled Jude to smother high thinkings under immediate needs. He had to get up, and seek for work, manual work; the only kind deemed by many of its professors to be work at all. Passing out into the streets on this errand he found that the colleges had treacherously changed their sympathetic countenances: some were stern; some had put on the look of family vaults above ground; something barbaric loomed in the masonries of all. The spirits of the great men had disappeared.

The numberless architectural pages around him he read, naturally, less as an artist-critic of their forms than as an artizan and comrade of the dead handicraftsmen whose muscles had actually executed those forms. He examined the mouldings, stroked them as one who knew their beginning, said they were difficult or easy in the working, had taken little or much time, were trying to the arm, or convenient to the tool.

What at night had been perfect and ideal was by day the more or less defective real. Cruelties, insults had, he perceived, been inflicted on the aged erections. The conditions of several moved him as he would have been moved by maimed sentient beings. They were wounded, broken, sloughing off their outer shape in the deadly struggle against years, weather, and man.

The rottenness of these historical documents reminded him that he was not, after all, hastening on to begin the morning practically as he had intended. He had come to work, and to live by work, and the morning had nearly gone. It was, in one sense, encouraging to think that in a place of crumbling stones there must be plenty of work for one of his trade to do in the business of renovation. He asked his way to the workyard of the stone-cutter whose name had been given him at Alfredston; and soon heard the familiar sound of the rubbers and chisels.

The yard was a little centre of regeneration. Here, with keen edges and smooth curves, were forms in the exact likeness of those he had seen abraded and time eaten on the walls. These were the ideas in modern prose which the lichened colleges presented in old poetry. Even some of those antiques might have been called prose when they were new. They had done nothing but wait, and had become poetical. How easy to the smallest building; how impossible to most men.

He asked for the foreman, and looked round among the new traceries, mullions, transoms, shafts, pinnacles, and battlements standing on the bankers half worked, or waiting to be removed. They were marked by precision, mathematical straightness, smoothness, exactitude: there in the old walls were the broken lines of the original idea; jagged curves, disdain of precision, irregularity, disarray.

For a moment there fell on Jude a true illumination; that here in the stone yard was a centre of effort as worthy as that dignified by the name of scholarly study within the noblest of the colleges. But he lost it under stress of his old idea. He would accept any employment which might be offered him on the strength of his late employer's recommendation; but he would accept it as a provisional thing only. This was his form of the modern vice of unrest.

The opening sentence introduces some of the key contrasting terms upon which the novel hinges. Necessity contrasts with choice, meditation with action, the actual with the phantasmal. Jude and Sue aspire to freedom and self-determination, but throughout the novel various forms of compulsion, some internal, others from the outside world, restrict their capacity to choose a particular course. Both are drawn to the ideal and imaginary: aunt Drusilla remarks that as children Jude and Sue tended to project phantasms beyond the physical realities of life, 'seeming to see things in the air' (p. 112). But the claims of the material world cannot be so readily dispelled. What is the value of ideals and aspirations in a world where survival is a daily struggle and hard toil a necessity?

Use of the word 'professors' is **ironic**. Jude is dazzled by his conception of the scholarly life led by professors within the university. The word 'professors' here, however, signifies not academics, but those who 'profess', or engage in, manual labour.

The **image** of colleges 'treacherously' changing 'their sympathetic countenances' is an instance of personification, the device of attributing human characteristics to the nonhuman world. It is used to indicate a change in Jude's perception of the Christminster environment. The buildings remain physically the same, but Jude projects his disappointment on to them and they assume a different guise within his mind. Knowledge of the world, in *Jude the Obscure*, is relative, not absolute. Interpretations vary as **points of view** change.

The intensity of Jude's desire to enter the university was externalised, on his arrival in Christminster, through his imaginative projection of the spirits of his intellectual heroes, peopling the nocturnal streets of the city. The 'mean bread-and-cheese question' has narrowed the focus of his desire to 'immediate needs', and the colleges now resemble tombs, housing grimly those stern figures. The classical learning, which earlier inspired Jude's ambition, has been ousted by 'something barbaric' in the appearance of the inhospitable city. The word 'barbarian' was originally applied to people who could not speak Greek, and were consequently considered uncivilised outsiders. It is **ironic** that Jude, who has striven to teach himself ancient Greek, but is nonetheless viewed as an uncivilised outsider by the Christminster institutions, should detect a barbaric aspect to the college buildings.

Jude conceives greatness in terms of intellectual achievement and the ability to transmit ideas to one's contemporaries and to posterity. The alternative is obscurity, remaining unknown in one's time, and leaving no trace of one's existence. That is Jude's lot. He has children, but they die before him. He leaves no written word, except an obscure inscription on the back of a milestone (see p. 73), and biblical texts copied on commission. In this passage, he reads the buildings as 'historical documents', but from the point of view of the anonymous artisan rather than a celebrated 'artist-critic'. His understanding of the mouldings is tactile rather than intellectual, the product of touch and craft rather than abstract analysis. Jude seems temporarily resigned to his status as a member of the skilled working class, rather than the educated middle class to whose life he has previously aspired. But he cannot for long overcome his infatuation with intellect and abstract thought.

Comprehension limited by dim perception, the condition of vision at night, is contrasted with the fuller understanding allowed by the illumination of daylight. What seemed 'perfect and ideal' when dimly grasped appears defective yet real when clearly seen. In the long term, Jude's perception of Christminster retains that ideal aspect which arises from partial understanding. In contrast, figures such as Arabella Donn and the physician Vilbert harbour no delusions; they see clearly but they never strive like Jude to see further. That is their strength and their limitation.

Thomas Hardy regularly employs animal **imagery** to create a sense that his characters are helpless victims, being pursued and tormented by an enemy they only partially comprehend. Here he uses a **metaphor** to extend the effect of such imagery to architecture. Buildings are said to be 'wounded', caught in a struggle against time, the natural elements and human abuse. Jude suffers similarly from the effects of history, material circumstances and human actions, is similarly 'maimed' and is similarly powerless. Renovation work is taking place. There is no comparable provision for Jude's regeneration, although for a while he comes to feel that Sue is fulfilling that function.

Thomas Hardy extends the metaphoric parallel he has drawn between architecture and written text. The mouldings in the stonecutter's yard are said to be 'modern prose' versions of the forms which appear as 'old poetry' on the college buildings. The contrast is between what is seen in stark factual terms, as carved stone, and what has accrued denser meaning, as historically enriched architectural feature. *Jude the Obscure* shows an individual life embedded within history, and shaped by the past as well as by present influences.

Thomas Hardy's training as an architect made him familiar with the technical vocabulary of stonemasonry. Reference here to 'traceries, mullions, transoms' and so on, indicates that those trained in this craft use a specialised language, just as scholars trained in philosophy or mathematics do. But although such terminology refers to forms, stonemasonry belongs to a material rather than an ideal world, and the 'precision' and 'exactitude' of the newly crafted artefacts will diminish with use. In a novel built upon tensions arising from the disparity of the physical and the ideal, even relatively durable architectural features are seen to fall away from 'the original idea' into 'irregularity' and 'disarray'.

Jude clings to 'his old idea' of pursuing a scholarly life amid abstractions, rather than settling for the tangible rewards of a practical life as a renovating worker in stone. He is susceptible to 'the modern vice of unrest'. This 'vice' is a refusal to accept limited horizons, an uprootedness from traditional ways of life, and a restless striving for some dimly perceived goal. It invariably involves subordination of the material world to some impalpable ideal (see Themes, on Ideal Forms & Material Reality).

TEXT 2   (from PART THIRD, CHAPTER I, PAGES 134–6)

She was something of a riddle to him, and he let the subject drift away. 'Shall we go and sit in the Cathedral?' he asked, when their meal was finished.

'Cathedral? Yes. Though I think I'd rather sit in a railway station,' she answered, a remnant of vexation still in her voice. 'That's the centre of town life now. The Cathedral has had its day!'

'How modern you are!'

'So would you be if you had lived so much in the Middle Ages as I have done these last few years! The Cathedral was a very good place four or five centuries ago; but it is played out now … I am not modern, either. I am more ancient than medievalism, if you only knew.'

Jude looked distressed.

'There – I won't say any more of that! she cried. 'Only you don't know how bad I am, from your point of view, or you wouldn't think so much of me, or care whether I was engaged or not. Now there's just time for us to walk round the Close, and then I must go in, or I shall be locked out for the night.'

He took her to the gate and they parted. Jude had a conviction that his unhappy visit to her on that sad night had precipitated this marriage engagement, and it did anything but add to his happiness. Her reproach had taken that shape, then, and not the shape of words. However, next day he set about seeking employment, which it was not so easy to get as at Christminster, there being, as a rule, less stone-cutting in progress in this quiet city, and hands being mostly permanent. But he edged himself in by degrees. His first work was some carving at the cemetery on the hill; and ultimately he became engaged on the labour he most desired – the Cathedral repairs, which were very extensive, the whole interior fittings having been swept away to be replaced by new.

It might be a labour of years to get it all done, and he had confidence enough in his own skill with the mallet and chisel to feel that it would be a matter of choice with himself how long he would stay.

The lodgings he took near the Close Gate would not have disgraced a curate, the rent representing a higher percentage on his wages than mechanics of any sort usually care to pay. His combined bed and sitting room was furnished with framed photographs of the rectories and deaneries at which his landlady had lived as trusted servant in her time, and the parlour downstairs bore a clock on the mantelpiece inscribed to the effect that it was presented to the same serious-minded woman by her fellow-servants on the occasion of her marriage. Jude added to the furniture of his room by unpacking photographs of the ecclesiastical carvings and monuments he had executed with his own hands; and he was deemed a satisfactory acquisition as tenant of the vacant apartment.

The topic under discussion at the start of this passage is Sue Bridehead's engagement to Richard Phillotson. Sue is said to be a riddle to Jude. He is trying to read her, but experiences great difficulty extracting clear meaning. Phillotson similarly comes to regard Sue as a puzzle. Both men believe this enigmatic woman can be deciphered, but she remains complex and mysterious. In this passage, Jude tries to interpret Sue's engagement as a reproach to him that has taken the shape of action 'and not the shape of words'.

Jude's faith in scholarship leads him to believe that close scrutiny of texts can deliver answers to life's questions, but although a book can offer a clear and persuasive line of argument, lived experience does not conform neatly to any theory. The material world is far messier than the realm of ideas. Critics have used analytical methods derived from psychology and from feminist theory to uncover the obscure motivation for Sue's unpredictable behaviour (see Contemporary Approaches). But no single theory resolves the riddle. *Jude the Obscure* is a novel that frustrates our desire for authoritative interpretations.

At the start of the novel we are told that the old church at Marygreen has been demolished and replaced by a new one. Here, we learn that the interior fittings of Christminster cathedral have been 'swept away, to be replaced by new'. In a characteristically radical gesture, Sue sweeps away the cathedral more fundamentally, as an outmoded concept which 'has had its day'. In its place she installs the railway station: 'That's the centre of town life now'. Historically there is some validity in her claim. The cathedral served a co-ordinating function for medieval society that the railway station increasingly assumed during the nineteenth century (see Historical Background, on Railways). But Sue's dismissal of the cathedral is primarily a **metonymy** for her rejection of Christian belief.

The cathedral, a vertical **symbol** of Christian aspiration to a life transcending the material world, has been superseded, Sue suggests, by the railway network, a horizontal symbol of modern mobility through the material world. Sue declares that she is 'bad' from Jude's orthodox

Christian **point of view**, yet she also rejects the notion that she is modern, in the material sense that the railways were modern in Victorian England. She is 'more ancient than medievalism', having steeped herself in the pagan thought of ancient Greece, especially the idealist philosophy of Plato as she has come to know it through the poetry of Percy Shelley (see Literary Background, on Shelley).

Sue will be locked out if she is late returning to the school where she is training to become a teacher. This threat of exclusion from an institution to which she has been admitted reflects **ironically** upon Jude's total exclusion from the educational institution to which he seeks access. Of course, Sue suffers educational disadvantages as a woman in this patriarchal society, just as Jude does as a working-class man (see Historical Background, on Education).

In Text 1, Thomas Hardy uses the word 'professors' to mean those who follow an occupation as manual workers. It is a **pun** on the more customary association of the word with academic work. We may detect a similar pun in Arabella's name 'Donn'; a 'don' is an academic member of staff, such as those who take part in the Christminster procession. In Text 2, we find that Jude, excluded from the university, edges his way 'by degrees' into employment as a stonecutter. This is perhaps another pun, alluding to academic degrees issued by the university. It might not have been Thomas Hardy's intention that this association should be made, but it is permissible for us to recognise in this ironic text the operation of irony at a verbal level, in the form of puns.

Photographs play a significant role in *Jude the Obscure*. They are a manifestation of modern technological ingenuity, but they also constitute a new way of remembering, even a new relationship with the past. Photographs externalise memory, preserving in material form images which would otherwise have been trapped within an individual's recollection. But although a photograph is itself an object, the image it captures invariably becomes an immaterial substitute for an experience that has passed. People and places alter, but in photographic images they appear changeless. Photographs occupy a curious position between the changing physical world and a timeless realm of immutable ideal forms.

The landlady has photographs of clerical houses where she has been a servant, and Jude has photographs of stonemasonry work which, after completion, has left his hands. The world around them changes, but these images seem to offer some form of stability and permanence. Jude and Phillotson cherish Sue's photograph because her actual person is evasive, continually slipping away from them, physically and conceptually. But although a photograph seems to preserve a moment, it actually registers distance in space and in time, absence and loss. This is nowhere more evident than when Jude finds his own framed image in a junk shop, jettisoned by Arabella as she departed for the other side of the world, leaving the past behind. She has no time for such immaterial substitutes, such consolatory illusions, as she has turned her attention fully to her immediate physical needs.

TEXT 3   (from PART SIXTH, CHAPTER 2, PAGES 336-7)

'Done because we are too menny.'

At sight of this Sue's nerves utterly gave way, an awful conviction that her discourse with the boy had been the main cause of the tragedy, throwing her into a convulsive agony which knew no abatement. They carried her away against her wish to a room on the lower floor; and there she lay, her slight figure shaken with her gasps, and her eyes staring at the ceiling, the woman of the house vainly trying to soothe her.

They could hear from this chamber the people moving about above, and she implored to be allowed to go back, and was only kept from doing so by the assurance that, if there were any hope, her presence might do harm, and the reminder that it was necessary to take care of herself lest she should endanger a life coming. Her inquiries were incessant, and at last Jude came down and told her that there was no hope. As soon as she could speak she informed him what she had said to the boy, and how she thought herself the cause of this.

'No,' said Jude. 'It was in his nature to do it. The doctor says there are such boys springing up amongst us – boys of a sort unknown in the last generation – the outcome of new views of life. They seem to see all its terrors before they are old enough to have staying power to resist them. He says it is the beginning of the coming universal wish not to live. He's an advanced man, the doctor: but he can give no consolation to –'

Jude had kept back his own grief on account of her; but he now broke down; and this stimulated Sue to efforts of sympathy which in some degree distracted her from her poignant self-reproach. When everybody was gone she was allowed to see the children.

The boy's face expressed the whole tale of their situation. On that little shape had converged all the inauspiciousness and shadow which had darkened the first union of Jude, and all the accidents, mistakes, fears, errors of the last. He was their nodal point, their focus, their expression in a single term. For the rashness of those parents he had groaned, for their ill-assortment he had quaked, and for the misfortunes of these he had died.

When the house was silent, and they could do nothing but await the coroner's inquest, a subdued, large, low voice spread into the air of the room from behind the heavy walls at the back.

'What is it?' said Sue, her spasmodic breathing suspended.

'The organ of the College chapel. The organist practising I suppose. It's the anthem from the seventy-third Psalm; "Truly God is loving unto Israel." '

She sobbed again. 'O my babies! They had done no harm! Why should they have been taken away, and not I!'

There was another stillness – broken at last by two persons in conversation somewhere without.

'They are talking about us, no doubt!' moaned Sue. ' "We are made a spectacle unto the world, and to angels, and to men!" '

Jude listened – 'No – they are not talking of us,' he said. They are two clergymen of different views, arguing about the eastward position.'

Then another silence, till she was seized with another uncontrollable fit of grief. 'There is something external to us which says, "You shan't!" First it said, "You shan't learn!" Then it said, "You shan't labour!" Now it says, "You shan't love!" '

Text 1 refers to the spirits of 'great' writers whom Jude has revered and dreamt of emulating. The only text of his own Jude leaves behind, however, is an obscure inscription on the back of a milestone. With crushing **irony**, Jude's son, Little Father Time, transmits a message to those he leaves behind when he commits suicide; its effect is not edifying but horrifying. The hand-written note declares that he has acted in this way 'because we are too menny'. Little Father Time's meagre education is indicated by his eccentric spelling.

Little Father Time perceives that Sue and Jude are struggling to provide for their children. By committing murder and taking his own life he believes he can ameliorate that situation. He cannot conceive that their grief will far outweigh the practical benefit of having fewer mouths to feed. His understanding is limited, yet he acts upon that understanding. These grotesque deaths constitute a perverse footnote to an animated nineteenth-century debate concerning population growth in relation to subsistence. It was stimulated initially by Thomas Malthus's *An Essay On the Principle of Population* (see Historical Background, on Thomas Malthus).

Sue is plunged into agonising despair by the perception that her discussion with the boy, and especially revelation of her current pregnancy, was the main cause of the 'tragedy'. The grotesqueness of Little Father Time's response to the conversation tests the limits of how we define **tragedy**. *The Life of Thomas Hardy*, an autobiography published as the work of the author's wife, Florence, contains his observation that 'if you blind yourself to the deeper issues of a tragedy you see a farce'.

The scene may appear tragic if we regard it as foreshadowing a general distaste for life, the spread of anti-life sentiments amongst human beings, rather than being an isolated and perverse incident. The doctor, an advanced thinker who figures only marginally but nonetheless offers a telling contrast to the itinerant quack Vilbert, says that 'it is the beginning of the coming universal wish not to live' (p. 337). This might conceivably be the eventual outcome of such self-consciousness and hypersensitivity as Jude and Sue manifest.

It appears that Little Father Time has exercised his will in committing murder and suicide, but there are suggestions in the novel that inherited characteristics to some extent determine his course of action. Aunt Drusilla wishes that young Jude were dead rather than troubling her, and Jude himself has moments when he wishes he had not been born. In Part First, Chapter 11, after walking on a frozen pond, Jude ponders: 'What was he reserved for? He supposed he was not a sufficiently dignified person for suicide' (p. 70). His son's suicide is entirely devoid of dignity.

A few pages later, Sue blames herself for explaining their situation to the child 'too obscurely' (p. 338). Yet she clings to grand abstractions such as Nature and Fate, rather than conceiving life in terms of human relationships. In this she differs dramatically from Arabella who is interested in life as it is lived through the senses. The narrator describes the appearance of Little Father Time's corpse in terms which may reflect Sue's perception of the dead child. Certainly the description conforms to the tendency Sue shares with Jude to subordinate physical reality to abstraction, and to read ideas into events. The boy's 'little shape' here assumes the portentousness of a 'nodal point' for the entire history of Jude's life with Arabella and with Sue. Specific ways in which particular causes have produced this effect are not identified, but the weighty pronouncement forcibly suggests the past's oppressively deterministic influence upon the unfolding present.

Thomas Hardy regularly uses the acoustic environment in this book to create ironic juxtapositions. At the end, a waltz from the joyful Christminster festivities is heard in the room where Jude's corpse lies. Here, as Sue and Jude sit in forlorn silence, the sound of an organ enters the room. The instrument's gravity might appear appropriate to this scene, but the music it plays, a Psalm affirming God's love, introduces a grim irony. Voices are also heard from outside, 'two clergymen of different views, arguing about the eastward position'. Once again point of view is an issue in the novel, but these representatives of the Church are expending their energy in debating a theological nicety, while Jude and Sue suffer the loss of their children in a bewildered and desperate state.

In *Jude the Obscure* religion is seen as a set of conventional forms offering temporary personal consolation rather than universal salvation. This is nowhere clearer than in Part Fifth, Chapter 7, where Arabella puts on an unconvincing show of piety following Cartlett's death. Her interest in religion is soon dispelled as her interest in Jude revives. The Bible is nonetheless quoted extensively. It was after all a cornerstone of elementary education in Victorian England.

Sue recalls the fate of the Apostles, 'made a spectacle unto the world, and to angels, and to men'. It is the case that she and Jude have come under public scrutiny on account of their unorthodox behaviour, especially as they have lived together unmarried with children. But the discomfort of being watched is heightened by the couple's intense self-consciousness. The unreflecting Arabella would not be troubled by such attention.

At this point Sue cannot believe in a benign God; rather she conceives 'something external to us', a devastating force which forms an insurmountable obstacle to their fulfilment and happiness. Whether it is called Nature's Law or Fate or Necessity, her sense of this impersonal force finally dispels her belief in individual freedom and the right to live by one's instincts. Before long, she turns to Christian piety as a way to restore meaning to her life. Jude, on the other hand, moves inexorably towards the culminating failure of his bleak life.

PART FIVE

BACKGROUND

HARDY'S LIFE & WORK

Thomas Hardy was born in the village of Higher Bockhampton, in Dorset, on 2 June 1840. His parents subsequently had another son and two daughters. Dorset, in the south-west of England, together with parts of its neighbouring counties, became the Wessex of Hardy's fiction, and his novels preserve elements of rural ways of life that were vanishing or had vanished when he was growing up.

Hardy remained very close to his mother Jemima, who died in 1904. His father Thomas, who died in 1892, was a builder and stonemason. After attending school in the village, then in the nearby town of Dorchester, Thomas Hardy became articled to a local architect in 1856, and later became his assistant. Raymond Williams, in' *The English Novel from Hardy to Dickens* (Chatto & Windus, 1970), suggests that this background, belonging neither to the labouring nor the landowning class, allowed Hardy to write of rural Wessex and its people with a singular mixture of detachment and passion. Hardy's training continued following his move to London as a draughtsman in 1862, and in 1867 he returned to Dorset as a practising architect. His knowledge of buildings, their construction and restoration forms an important component of *Jude the Obscure*, elaborating Jude's character and the Christminster environment.

In 1874, Thomas Hardy married Emma Lavinia Gifford. They moved to London four years later. During 1880, Hardy was seriously ill for several months. In 1881 the couple returned to Dorset, and in 1885 they settled at Max Gate, a house which Hardy had designed and his brother Henry had built, on the outskirts of Dorchester. The couple had no children. Although Hardy has often been viewed as a regional novelist, his awareness of London life is discernibly a factor in *Jude the Obscure*, where significant contrasts are established between urban and rural conditions.

While he was writing *Jude the Obscure*, a novel which questions conventional views of marriage, Thomas Hardy's relationship with his wife deteriorated. The couple remained at Max Gate, but lived separate lives until Emma's death in November 1911. Hardy had close friendships and some emotional involvement with other women during this period.

In February 1914 he married Florence Emily Dugdale, whom he had met in 1905, and who had worked as his secretary. Her book, *The Life of Thomas Hardy*, actually written by Hardy himself, was published after the novelist's death.

Thomas Hardy died on 11 January 1928, aged eighty-eight. He had become one of England's most eminent literary figures, receiving the Order of Merit in 1910. His ashes were buried in Poets' Corner, Westminster Abbey. His heart was interred in his first wife Emma's grave, in the churchyard at Stinsford, Dorset.

Biographers have served Thomas Hardy well. Notable accounts are Robert Gittings's two volumes, *Young Thomas Hardy* (Penguin, 1978) and *The Older Hardy* (Penguin, 1980), Michael Millgate's *Thomas Hardy: A Biography* (Oxford University Press, 1982), and Martin Seymour-Smith's *Hardy* (Bloomsbury, 1994). *The Collected Letters of Thomas Hardy* have been edited in seven volumes by Richard Purdy and Michael Millgate (Oxford University Press, 1978–88).

His writings

Thomas Hardy achieved popularity as a novelist skilled in evoking rural life. This aptitude is apparent in the simple charm of his second novel, *Under the Greenwood Tree* (1872); his first published novel, *Desperate Remedies*, appeared in 1871. The success of his fourth book, *Far from the Madding Crowd* (1874), persuaded Thomas Hardy to become a full-time writer. It also marked an advance in technical accomplishment, with some reviewers comparing it to the work of the highly respected novelist George Eliot (1819–80).

Most sustained critical attention has been reserved for later works which are often classed as 'the tragic novels'. These are *The Return of the Native* (1878), *The Mayor of Casterbridge* (1886), *Tess of the d'Urbervilles* (1891), and *Jude the Obscure* (1896). *Jude the Obscure* appears something of a departure in its shift of focus from rural Wessex to the city of Christminster. It also seems stylistically distinct, with more blatant artifice and distortion in its treatment of character and plot. But there are thematic continuities. Before creating Jude Fawley, and notably in Tess Durbeyfield, Thomas Hardy had created protagonists who are displaced from their social background, uprooted from the traditional life of their community and their class, and cast into a far less predictable, much more volatile social world. These characters reflect larger changes in the composition and structure of English society during the course of the nineteenth century, with a major shift from the rural to the urban environment, and new relationships emerging between men and women and between social classes.

Jude the Obscure also resembles *Tess of the d'Urbervilles* in its frank treatment of religious scepticism and unconventional conduct between the sexes. Victorian moral propriety was offended, and both novels generated voluble protest. Thomas Hardy claimed that this hostility persuaded him to abandon the novel as a literary form and to turn to poetry. In fact, he had started to write poetry in the late 1850s, and he seems to have always considered himself primarily a poet. He published several collections, starting with *Wessex Poems* (1898) and *Poems of the Past and the Present* (1901). A major dramatic epic in verse, *The Dynasts* appeared between 1904 and 1908. Many critics consider Thomas Hardy's poetry to be a still greater achievement than his novels.

HISTORICAL BACKGROUND

THOMAS MALTHUS

Little Father Time's suicide note indicates that he has taken his life 'because we are too menny'. His understanding is that the family has grown too large, and that Sue and Jude are struggling to provide for their children. The issue of population growth in relation to subsistence was a topic of keen debate during the nineteenth century, stimulated initially by *An Essay On the Principle of Population* (1798; revised 1830) by Thomas Malthus (1766–1834), who subsequently became Britain's first professor of political economy.

Malthus argued that population growth is a geometrical progression, while advances in production of the means to sustain life follow an arithmetical progression. So, population constantly outstrips subsistence. He concluded that a range of checks, such as disease, war and pestilence, operate as a kind of natural law to restore balance between human numbers and available resources. Malthus believed that large cities were unwholesome environments, incubating misery and vice, so the growth of urban populations actually became a form of check upon the population overall.

Thomas Hardy makes no direct reference to Malthus in *Jude the Obscure*, but in *Tess of the d'Urbervilles* (1891), Phase the First, Chapter 5, he uses the adjective Malthusian to describe Tess Durbeyfield's critical attitude towards her mother 'for thoughtlessly giving her so many little sisters and brothers'. Little Father Time's response to Sue's final pregnancy is a grotesque intensification of Tess's reaction, and by committing murder then suicide the boy becomes a perverse incarnation of Malthusian theory.

THE DECLINING IMPORTANCE OF AGRICULTURE

Agriculture was for centuries the foundation and backdrop for English social life. By the middle of the nineteenth century it no longer dominated the nation's economy, although it remained a major element within it, supplying food for the growing population of urban areas. During the decade in which *Jude the Obscure* was written, the closing years of that century, agriculture lost its place as the largest source of employment, being superseded by transport and metal industries.

'Pig-jobbing', as practised by Arabella Donn's family, is said in the novel to be no longer economically viable. Ease of transportation and improvements in processing technology had resulted in such local employment being organised more efficiently in towns. The Donns respond dramatically by emigrating to Australia, a vivid illustration of that relocation which became increasingly necessary for a significant number of the rural population. Jude trains as a stonemason in order to make himself employable in the city; he equates a return to village life with personal failure.

EDUCATION

Late in the nineteenth century, the universities of Oxford and Cambridge remained bastions of social privilege, serving the interests of the nation's ruling elite. In 1873, however, the University of Cambridge initiated the university extension movement, granting access to some men from the lower social classes. Oxford, upon which Thomas Hardy's Christminster is based, followed in 1875, and the process gained momentum throughout the mid-1880s. Jude Fawley is aware of this widening access, but recognises that this historical development has occurred too late for him. The extension movement was an important step towards establishing higher educational places for women.

Sue Bridehead, whose intellect is more than a match for both Jude and Richard Phillotson, gains access to a training-school, which aims to equip her for a subordinate role as a teaching assistant. She harbours no dream comparable to Jude's of entering the university, because rigorous exclusion of women made even the dream untenable. Her own frustration fires Sue's critical assessment of the limits to Jude's comprehension: 'He still thinks it a great centre of high and fearless thought, instead of what it is, a nest of commonplace schoolmasters whose characteristic is timid obsequiousness to tradition' (p. 313).

LOSS OF RELIGIOUS FAITH

Thomas Hardy, raised a Christian and trained as an ecclesiastical architect, became agnostic while in his twenties. During the second half of the nineteenth century, many educated members of the middle class found themselves confronted with arguments that challenged the authority of orthodox Christianity. These arose from a variety of sources, but the geological discoveries of Sir Charles Lyell (1797–1875) and the evolutionary theory expounded by Charles Darwin (1809–82) were amongst the most unsettling rivals to biblical accounts.

In *Jude the Obscure* the challenge is not from scientific thinking but is posed by radical philosophy and by theological revisionism which subjected the Bible to unfamiliar critical exposition. Sue Bridehead, although an outsider to the university, understands that 'at present intellect in Christminster is pushing one way, and religion the other; and so they stand stockstill, like two rams butting each other' (p. 151). She has additionally come under the atheistical influence of the early nineteenth-century poet Shelley (see Literary Background, on Shelley).

Sue's reading, coupled with a rebellious temperament, leads her to reject orthodox Christian belief. In its place she turns to the religion and philosophy of ancient Greece, to the deities Venus and Apollo, and to the philosophy of Plato (*c.*429–347BC). Jude increasingly falls under the influence of her scepticism, and has lost his faith entirely by the point when Sue forces herself back to piety as an act of overt self-suppression. Above and beyond these individual cases, Thomas Hardy creates in *Jude the Obscure* an oppressive sense that modern people are spiritually as well as physically uprooted and adrift. The novel is laden with biblical allusions and quotations, yet it depicts a world in which demonstrations of religious belief are largely 'a luxury of the emotional and leisured classes' (p. 91).

An atmosphere of deep pessimism prevails. Jude becomes dismissive not only of Christian belief but of all forms of received wisdom, including conventions of social organisation. He finds himself 'in a chaos of principles – groping in the dark – acting by instinct and not after example'. His 'fixed opinions' drop away until his 'present rule of life' consists merely of 'following inclinations which do me and nobody else any harm, and actually give pleasure to those I love best' (p. 327). The intention is benign, but the consequences to Jude are disastrous.

A 'chaos of principles' precipitates a similarly catastrophic outcome in certain early twentieth-century fictions, such as *Heart of Darkness* (1902) by Joseph Conrad (1857–1924), and *The Good Soldier* (1915) by Ford Madox Ford (1873–1939). Both share the gloomy perception that codes of social conduct have lost their credibility to the point where individuals are thrown back upon their own instincts, and may perish as a consequence.

RAILWAYS

'The Cathedral has had its day!' declares Sue Bridehead, the railway station is 'the centre of the town life now' (p. 135). Her remark is astute, for as the influence of Christianity waned in the late nineteenth century, the development of an extensive railway network had a dramatic impact upon social and economic relationships. Jobs which for centuries had been performed in villages were now executed more efficiently in towns, and the effect of this upon rural lifestyles and customs was immense.

Seventeen thousand miles of railways were constructed in Britain between 1830 and 1880, extending from city centres into previously isolated rural areas. Rail travel speeded up the pace of life dramatically. Metropolitan influence filtered far more rapidly into the countryside, hastening a demographic shift into urban regions, and contributing to that psychology of restless mobility which pervades *Jude the Obscure*.

The railway looms large in the novel; 'the screaming of the trains' has become a feature of rural Wessex (p. 137), an audible **symbol** of progress and the shaping power of industrial processes. The electric telegraph (mentioned on p. 207), a communications technology closely associated with the spread of rail, compounds the sense that human ingenuity is triumphing over space and diminishing distance. This has the physical consequence of enabling Arabella and her husband, Cartlett, to travel at speed and without difficulty from London to attend the Great Wessex Agricultural Show. It also forms an **ironic** counterpoint to Jude's dream of social mobility, which runs constantly into insurmountable obstacles. Christminster is initially a distant vision, but even when he lives in the heart of that city, the Christminster to which Jude aspired remains remote from him.

LITERARY BACKGROUND

SHELLEY

There are references to numerous poets in *Jude the Obscure*, but allusions to Percy Bysshe Shelley (1792–1822) carry a special resonance, given the novel's concern with issues of class, education, and unorthodox social and religious views. Shelley, a member of the English upper classes but also a political radical, attended Oxford, the university upon which Hardy's Christminster is based, and was expelled for writing an atheistical pamphlet.

More directly relevant to the novel is the neo-Platonic philosophy which informed Shelley's poetry. Plato was a Greek philosopher who asserted that the material world is illusory, and that reality resides in an ideal realm, accessible to philosophy but incapable of being apprehended through the physical senses. It is appropriate that Sue Bridehead, with her aversion to physicality and attraction to ideals, is a reader of Shelley. In particular she quotes his poem 'Epipsychidion' (1821). Its Greek title means 'little soul within a soul', signalling an ideal and immaterial form of love to which Sue and Jude at times aspire.

In one of the notes to his poem 'Queen Mab' (1813) Shelley expressed his distaste for legal marriage in terms which seem to be echoed by Sue. The essence of his argument was that 'love withers under constraint'. He equated religion and morality, as they were understood by his contemporaries, with misery and servitude.

THE NINETEENTH-CENTURY NOVEL

The novel in English was established early in the eighteenth century by Daniel Defoe (1660–1731), but in the nineteenth century it burgeoned as a literary form, achieving immense popularity through writers like Charles Dickens (1812–70) and Anthony Trollope (1815–82), and acquiring greater technical sophistication in the hands of authors such as George Eliot (1819–80) and George Meredith (1828–1909). Many novels were initially published in serial form in weekly or monthly periodicals. As bound books their standard format, from the time of Sir Walter Scott (1771–1832) onwards, was the three-volume work, so many nineteenth-century novels are of considerable length.

Nineteenth-century novels were predominantly 'realist' works, that is, they represented individual characters and social groups as knowable entities. As novelists strived for greater psychological complexity, encompassing ambiguous and oblique motivation, this criterion of knowability came under some strain. In *Jude the Obscure*, Sue Bridehead remains puzzling and mysterious even to those who know her most intimately. She does not conform to the representational requirements of classic realist fiction, but anticipates the more indirect and unstable modes of characterisation found in the mature works of twentieth-century writers such as Virginia Woolf (1882–1941) and D.H. Lawrence (1885–1930).

The very obvious contrivances of plot in *Jude the Obscure*, the coincidences and almost geometrical correspondences between the courses of characters' lives, raise the inconspicuous artifice of realist fiction into unsettling visibility. This novel's **ironic** variations on nineteenth-century novelistic convention suggest that *Jude the Obscure* might be aligned more appropriately with the innovative fiction of the generation that followed Thomas Hardy.

PART SIX

CRITICAL HISTORY & BROADER PERSPECTIVES

RECEPTION & EARLY CRITICAL VIEWS

Thomas Hardy's frank representation of individuals unable to accept conventional social values made his fiction controversial. As his later work grew bolder in addressing sensitive issues, publishers and editors became increasingly nervous of adverse responses from readers seeking to uphold late Victorian moral prejudices. Episodes in *The Mayor of Casterbridge* (1886) and *Tess of the d'Urbervilles* (1891) had to be amended before they were accepted for serial publication in magazines.

Harper's New Monthly Magazine agreed to serialise *Jude the Obscure* only if it caused no offence. Thomas Hardy did not abide by that initial undertaking, however, and in order to secure serial publication he had to make numerous modifications, cloaking the novel's concern with sexual matters. For example, Arabella's ploy of feigning pregnancy to trick Jude into marriage was altered to a less convincing kind of pressure involving a former lover who now wished to become her husband.

The offending passages were restored for publication in book form, and this led to hostile reviews that found the novel immoral. Thomas Hardy claimed (perhaps disingenuously) that this adverse response, outweighing the praise the novel received, contributed to his decision to abandon the novel form. He subsequently wrote only poetry. *The Well-Beloved* (1897), his last novel to be published was actually written prior to *Jude the Obscure*.

Contemporary reviews are collected in R.G. Cox's *Thomas Hardy: The Critical Heritage* (Routledge, 1970).

CRITICAL RESPONSES

Early critical responses to Thomas Hardy's fiction focused upon his creation of memorable figures, and on his delineation of Wessex, that region in the south-west of England which has come to be known as 'Hardy country'. *Jude the Obscure* is untypical in the extent of its departure from that rural setting. This strand of criticism, exemplified by F.

Manning's essay 'Novels of Character and Environment', published in the *Spectator* in 1912, was generally appreciative. But it also prepared the ground for F.R. Leavis's dismissive evaluation of the novelist, in his influential book, *The Great Tradition* (1948), as 'a provincial manufacturer' of 'heavy' fictions.

In 1914, the novelist D.H. Lawrence published his *Study of Thomas Hardy*, a stimulating yet idiosyncratic appraisal, which acknowledges the vitality of characterisation that produced Arabella Donn, and draws attention to Thomas Hardy's dissatisfaction with received social conventions and the demands of conformity. Lawrence suggests that Jude Fawley is unusual amongst Hardy's characters in the deliberateness with which he pursues his particular course of action. Lawrence identifies the tragic element in Thomas Hardy's writing as the inevitability with which characters who have broken free from social constraints then perish as a consequence. For Lawrence this duality, recognising the need for individuals to seek fulfilment beyond conformity, yet condemning them to suffer for doing so, is a flaw in Hardy's vision.

E.M. Forster and Virginia Woolf, two other major twentieth-century novelists, also responded to the power of Thomas Hardy's writing. Forster, in his book *Aspects of the Novel* (1927), concedes that he is drawn to Hardy's fiction in spite of reservations. Most serious is the fact that his characters are often dominated by plot. Forster cherished individual liberty, but in Hardy's fiction he found freedom to act too often displaced by the determining influence of impersonal forces. In *Jude the Obscure* especially, Forster found that Hardy's emphatic patterning of cause and effect stifled his characters.

Virginia Woolf's essay, 'The Novels of Thomas Hardy', written in 1928, and subsequently collected in *The Common Reader*, identifies an elemental quality in Hardy's most striking characters, making them simultaneously individuals and types. As individuals they help sustain credible narratives, while as types they engage our sympathetic recognition that we share, or have the common capacity to share, aspects of their character. Woolf discerns 'the poet's gift' in this capacity to balance the particular and the universal. Woolf finds *Jude the Obscure* 'the most painful' of Hardy's novels in its relentless pessimism, but the book's 'misery', she suggests, is overwhelming rather than tragic in effect, because a narrowly argued 'case against society' is too prominent.

Thomas Hardy's reputation as a major novelist was promoted by surveys such as David Cecil's *Hardy the Novelist* (1943), and Douglas Brown's *Thomas Hardy* (1954). More incisive analysis arrived with a series of studies that foregrounded formal issues. Jean Brooks's *Thomas Hardy: The Poetic Structure* (Elek Books, 1971) is a landmark of this kind of critical approach, examining the novels as composed structures rather than mirrors held up to reflect life. In the light of this approach, distortions and contrivances which might be considered flaws in Thomas Hardy's fiction can be seen as elements of design, the legitimate artifice of patterned prose. This formal emphasis can also be found in later studies such as Peter Casagrande's *Unity in Hardy's Novels: 'Repetitive Symmetries'* (Macmillan, 1982).

More recently, textual scholars, such as Simon Gatrell in *Hardy the Creator* (Clarendon Press, 1988), have followed the novels from their conception, through manuscript and into print, illuminating the author's acts of composition and revision.

Rosemary Sumner's *Thomas Hardy: Psychological Novelist* (Macmillan, 1981) was an important reassessment of the fiction, considering Thomas Hardy as a writer who moved away from conventional modes of characterisation found in earlier Victorian novels, and anticipated the psychoanalytical insights of Sigmund Freud (1856–1939) and his followers. Sumner discusses Sue's psychological complexity in relation to neurosis arising from sexual repression, and argues that *Jude the Obscure* forms an indictment of a sexually restrictive society. Another notable application of the psychological approach is Rosemary Morgan's *Women and Sexuality in the Novels of Thomas Hardy* (Routledge, 1988).

Other critics have looked at more material aspects of Thomas Hardy's concern with social and historical processes. The Marxist critic Raymond Williams wrote suggestively on this broader picture in *The English Novel from Dickens to Lawrence* (Chatto & Windus, 1970). Peter Widdowson's *Hardy in History: A Study in Literary Sociology* (Routledge, 1989) offers a more wide-ranging consideration.

Peter Widdowson's *Thomas Hardy* (Northcote House, Writers And Their Work, 1996) is a critical overview of Hardy's work and his place in literary history. Widdowson argues that despite the fact that the 'Preface' to *Jude the Obscure* affirms the novel's tragic status, the way the novel is written, its 'anti-realism', undermines such a claim. Widdowson suggests that we should view the novel as a **satire** addressing social injustice. Another example of critical concern with generic classification is R.P. Draper's essay 'Hardy's Comic Tragedy' (1990), reprinted in his revised edition of *Thomas Hardy: The Tragic Novels* Casebook Series (Macmillan, 1991). Draper links *Jude the Obscure* to eighteenth-century **mock-heroic** literature.

The proximity of tragedy and **farce** in *Jude the Obscure* has often been noted, and the novel's failure to make clear distinction between elevated topics and low **comedy** has been considered a lapse from good taste. John Goode, in *Thomas Hardy: The Offensive Truth* (Blackwell, 1988) takes this to be a strength of the novel. Goode reads the novel's inclination towards the **grotesque** as a calculated tactical blow against the received opinions and conformist attitudes of respectable readers. Another critic who has sought to dislodge the kind of reservations expressed by D.H. Lawrence is George Wotton, who in *Thomas Hardy: Towards a Materialist Criticism* (Gill & Macmillan, 1985) argues that *Jude the Obscure* is an effectively subversive novel which reflects in its writing social contradictions prevailing at the time it was produced.

Feminist analysis has made an especially fruitful contribution to Hardy criticism, revealing strengths and blindspots in the novelist's representation of women hemmed in by patriarchal assumptions. Notable examples are Penny Boumelha's *Thomas Hardy and Women: Sexual Ideology and Narrative Form* (Harvester Press, 1982) and Patricia Ingham's *Thomas Hardy: A Feminist Reading* (Harvester Wheatsheaf, 1989).

A useful selection of critical documents has been assembled by Penny Boumelha in *Jude the Obscure*, New Casebooks (Macmillan, 2000).

CONTEMPORARY APPROACHES

FEMINIST

A cabman mistreats his horse in Christminster and Jude remarks on the **irony** that such cruelty can occur at the gates of a college in 'the most religious and educational city in the world' (p. 328). Jude senses that 'there is something wrong somewhere in our social formulas' but cannot offer fuller diagnosis (p. 327). Feminist critics have performed the kind of analysis of which Jude was incapable, disclosing the ethical and political shortcomings of a patriarchal social order governed by conventionally masculine values that foster injustice and cruelty.

Feminist critics have used Thomas Hardy's own discontent with conventional attitudes towards marriage and the social status of women as a platform for their critique. This has involved disclosure of blindspots and contradictions within Hardy's critical position. It seems that he would have been open to such criticism. In his 1912 'Postscript' to the Wessex Edition of *Jude the Obscure*, he noted that one of the book's initial reviewers identified Sue Bridehead as a new type then emerging, 'the woman of the feminist movement'. Hardy neither confirms nor denies this; rather he concedes that 'there can be more in a book than the author consciously puts there' (p. 468).

Sue has proven a particularly attractive figure in her initial refusal to conform to stereotypical expectations. She evades Phillotson's perception of her as a little girl, and Jude's vision of her as a divine creature. She resists the subordinate role of wife, and the domestic confinement that expected of middle-class Victorians. She complains that the Church views her as an object to be given 'like a she-ass or she-goat, or any other domestic animal' (p. 170). She leaps from a window to escape the sexual demands she expects her husband to make. Sue desires to transcend her circumstances, rather than be bound by them. Although she gains admission to a training-school for teachers, she remains excluded, as a woman, from university education. Sue sees the school as a hybrid of nunnery and prison, and she breaks free from it.

Yet, despite her persistent bids for freedom, Sue ends up effectively buried alive as Phillotson's wife in Marygreen. Her fate illustrates the persistence of patriarchal injustice in a way that some happier ending would not achieve. It is a sign of work to be done.

Sophisticated feminist readings can be found in Penny Boumelha's *Thomas Hardy and Women: Sexual Ideology and Narrative Form* (Harvester Press, 1982), Patricia Ingham's *Thomas Hardy: A Feminist Reading* (Harvester Wheatsheaf, 1989), Marjorie Garson's *Hardy's Fables of Integrity: Woman, Body, Text* (Oxford University Press, 1991), and *The*

Sense of Sex: Feminist Perspectives on Hardy (University of Illinois Press, 1993) edited by Margaret R. Higgonet.

STRUCTURALIST

In a letter to the critic Edmund Gosse (1849–1928) Thomas Hardy observed that 'the book is all contrasts'. These contrasts make *Jude the Obscure* particularly amenable to a structuralist reading. The term 'structuralism' encompasses a range of critical practices which take their lead from the linguistic theories of Ferdinand de Saussure (1857–1913).

Saussure argued that language produces meaning not through reference to the world beyond language, but through differences with the language system itself. So, 'cat' means what it does because it is not 'bat', 'fat', 'can', 'cut', or any other word. When we hear or see the word 'cat' a concept springs immediately to mind. It is not a specific cat, but an idea of 'cat'. Similarly, encountering the word 'fate', a concept springs to mind. You could not point to 'fate' in the world around you, but the word has meaning because it is not, for example, 'hate', 'late', or 'rate'.

This may seem a strange way to conceive of language, but it becomes more readily comprehensible if we use the analogy of a game. Saussure compared language to chess, which has its own rules and meanings without referring to the world beyond the board and the pieces. The relationships between the pieces generate structures of meaning. In football, the ball in the back of the net means a goal. It acquires that meaning simply because it is different from the ball outside the net.

A structuralist reading of *Jude the Obscure* might point to ways in which meaning is produced not through reference to the world beyond the text, but through a structure of differences within it. The meaning of Arabella's sensuality is generated through its difference to Jude's intellectual aspirations, or to Sue's chasteness. The difference between Jude's age and Phillotson's age generates meaning when they become rivals for Sue's love. The urban assumes meaning in relation to the rural. The meaning of Christian values in this novel arises from their difference to the unbelief of modern scepticism, or to the pagan values of ancient Greece, as when Sue enters 'with her heathen load into the most Christian city in the country' (p. 94).

A much more refined structuralist reading, focusing upon contrasts between ideal and real, can be found in J. Hillis Miller's *Thomas Hardy: Distance and Desire* (Oxford University Press, 1970).

PSYCHOLOGICAL

Sue Bridehead affirms that 'some of the most passionately erotic poets have been the most self-contained in their daily lives' (p. 149). Sigmund Freud (1856–1939) later used the term 'sublimation' to identify this phenomenon, whereby repressed sexual impulses are channelled as creative energy into the production of works of art. Freud developed an elaborate theory of psychoanalysis which argued that human beings have the capacity to repress impulses, predominantly violent or sexual, which threaten to disrupt the integrity of the self, or of the social group.

These repressed urges and desires occupy the unconscious part of the self, beyond our conscious awareness, yet affecting our behaviour in unsuspected ways. Freud said that these repressed impulses must be released in some form: for example, through dreams, slips of the tongue, misplacing of objects, or through sublimation into art. If no alternative form of release is available, they will emerge as symptoms of mental illness. Although Sue identifies a correspondence between chastity and creativity in the work of certain poets, her own aversion to sexual contact suggests a pathological condition, producing only misery for herself and for Phillotson and Jude. This pathology should not, however, be narrowly attributed to Sue, but should be seen in the context of social conditions which have expanded her horizons, yet denied her access to a more fulfilling intellectual life.

Rosemary Sumner, in her book *Thomas Hardy: Psychological Novelist* (Macmillan, 1981) cites a story told by Freud in 1917, involving two young women: one has limited horizons, is sexually active, marries young, and feels no anxiety about her situation; the other is more highly educated, and represses her sexual impulses in accordance with ideals of purity and abstinence. As Sumner points out, these young women correspond neatly to Arabella and Sue. Sue is more refined ethically and intellectually, but that very refinement creates conflict with her sexual nature. It is worth remembering that Hardy was writing at a time when the very existence of women's sexuality was more or less denied by the

PSYCHOLOGICAL continued

Victorian middle classes. That makes the psychological complexity of his portrayal of Sue all the more remarkable.

Sumner suggests that Sue conforms to Freud's type of the narcissist, whose need is to be loved rather than to love, and consequently causes her lovers to doubt her love, and to complain of her puzzling nature. This may be read as Sue's unconscious response to the fact that her intellectual and spiritual aspirations have no means to achieve fulfilment. She seeks to become, instead, her own ideal.

Sumner also discerns masochism in Sue's self-sacrificial acts, which turn upon herself, narcissistically, the sadistic tendencies she has displayed in her relationships with Jude and Phillotson, both of whom feel tortured by her. Surrendering herself sexually to Phillotson, whom she finds physically repulsive, is her ultimate act of masochistic self-punishment, surrendering to sex drives that terrify her.

Freud's theories have been disputed and, in some cases, discredited, but they do allow us to appreciate that Thomas Hardy, in advance of Freud, was registering in his fiction a complex understanding of human behaviour which challenged long-held assumptions about the capacity of human beings to attain self-knowledge.

World events	Hardy's life	Literary events
1798 Thomas Malthus, *An Essay on the Principle of Population*		**1798-1844** Heyday of British Romantic Movement
		1821 Percy Bysshe Shelley, 'Epipsychidion'
1830-3 Charles Lyell, *Principles of Geology*		**1832** Death of Sir Walter Scott
1834 Union workhouses established; transportation of Tolpuddle martyrs to Australia		**1834** Harrison Ainsworth, *Rookwood*
1837 Accession of Queen Victoria		
1838 Formation of Anti-Corn Law League		
	1839 Thomas Hardy, mason, marries Jemima, cook	
	1840 Birth of **Thomas Hardy**, their son, at Higher Bockhampton, Dorset	**1840** Birth of Emile Zola
		1844 William Barnes, *Poems of Rural Life in the Dorset Dialect*
1846 Repeal of Corn Laws		
1847 Railway comes to Dorchester		
	1848 Attends village school	**1848** Harrison Ainsworth, *The Lancashire Witches;* birth of Richard Jefferies
		1850 Birth of Guy de Maupassant; death of Wordsworth; Nathaniel Hawthorne, *The Scarlet Letter*
1851 The Great Exhibition shows first reaping and threshing machines		
1854-6 Crimean War		**1854** Sarah Grand, writer and feminist born
		1855 Death of Charlotte Brontë; Olive Schreiner, South African writer and feminist born

World events	Hardy's life	Literary events
	1856-62 Apprenticed to architect John Hicks; witnesses public hanging of Martha Brown, Dorchester	
1857 Divorce Act		**1857** Gustave Flaubert, *Madame Bovary*
		1859 Charles Darwin, *On the Origin of Species*
		1860 George Eliot, *The Mill on the Floss*
		1861 Dickens, *Great Expectations;* Eliot, *Silas Marner*
	1862-67 Works in London as architect; begins to lose religious faith	
		1866 Dostoevsky, *Crime and Punishment*
	1867 Returns to Dorchester to work for Hicks; begins working on *The Poor Man and the Lady*	
	1869 Moves to Weymouth to work for architect Crickmay; begins writing *Desperate Remedies*	
1870 Foster's Education Act; elementary education for all; from hereon de-population of Dorset countryside	**1870** Restoring St Juliot's church, north Cornwall, Hardy meets his future wife, Emma Lavinia Gifford	
	1871 Publishes *Desperate Remedies*	**1871-2** Eliot, *Middlemarch*
	1872 Publishes *A Pair of Blue Eyes; Under the Greenwood Tree*	
	1873 *Far from the Madding Crowd* serialised	**1873** John Stuart Mill dies
1874-80 Disraeli Prime Minister	**1874** Marries Emma	

World events	Hardy's life	Literary events
	1876 They go to live at Sturminster Newton; *The Hand of Ethelberta* published	
		1877 Henry James, *The American*
	1878 *The Return of the Native*	**1878** Leo Tolstoy, *Anna Karenina*
	1880 *The Trumpet Major;* very ill for six months	**1880** Richard Jefferies, *Hodge and his Masters;* Maupassant, *Boule de Suif*
		1881 Jefferies, *Toilers of the Field*
		1882 Anthony Trollope dies
	1883 'The Dorsetshire Labourer'	
1884 Foundation of Fabian Society		**1884** Jefferies, *The Dewy Morn*
1885 Siege of Khartoum		**1885** George Meredith, *Diana of the Crossways*
1886 Six 'Jack the Ripper' murders, east London	**1886** *The Mayor of Casterbridge*	
	1887 *The Woodlanders*	**1887** Emile Zola, *La Terre (Earth)*
		1890 Henrik Ibsen, *Hedda Gabler*
1891 Education made free in England	**1891** *Tess of the d'Urbervilles* first serialised edition	
	1895 *Jude the Obscure;* relationship with Emma deteriorates	
	1898 *Wessex Poems*	
1899-1902 Boer War		
	1904 *The Dynasts*	
	1910 Awarded Order of Merit, after declining knighthood	
	1912 Death of Emma	
1914-18 First World War	**1914** Marries Florence Emily Dugdale, his secretary	
	1915 Mary, Hardy's sister, dies	
	1928 Death of Thomas Hardy	

caricature grotesque rendering of character, achieved through exaggeration of distinctive traits

comedy broad category, characterised by representation of the lighter side of life

dialect mode of speech peculiar to a particular region or social group

epigraph a quotation placed at the start of a book or a chapter, having some relevance to its contents

epithet word or phrase used as an adjective to convey some attribute of its object

farce low comedy presenting ludicrous situations

figurative form of expression that departs from basic requirements of simple communication, especially through the use of metaphor and simile

grotesque deliberate distortion intended to shock or satirise

image a word-picture, registering a strong impression of some scene or object

imagery figurative language, or words which refer to objects or qualities which appeal to the senses and feelings

irony irony arises when one thing is said, but another is understood, or when the significance of an event can be read in terms that are at odds with its apparent meaning

metaphor describing one thing as being another thing in order to highlight a particular quality which both share

metonymy referring to a thing by means of an attribute it possesses or by a quality associated with it

mock-heroic mode of writing which addresses a trivial subject with inappropriate grandeur to comic effect

omniscient narrator story-teller with total Godlike knowledge of the characters and their actions

pathetic fallacy term coined by critic John Ruskin (1819–1900) referring to the literary practice of equating the writer's or a character's mood with the surrounding environment, as when rage is mirrored in a storm

point of view position from which an utterance is delivered or an observation is made

pun a play on words, reliant upon recognition of more than one meaning attaching to a single word

realism or **realist fiction** fiction that proceeds from the assumption that characters and communities can be known, and that such knowledge may be conveyed through the medium of language

satire writing which exposes and ridicules the follies and frailties of human beings

simile a kind of metaphoric writing in which one thing is said to be like another thing

symbol an image that represents something else, by analogy or association

tragedy, tragic writing in which the career and downfall of an individual is traced with appropriate seriousness, illustrating both the capacities and the limitations of human life

AUTHOR OF THIS NOTE

Dr Julian Cowley taught English at King's College London before joining the University of Luton, where he is Senior Lecturer in Literary Studies.

York Notes Advanced (£3.99 each)

Margaret Atwood
Cat's Eye

Margaret Atwood
The Handmaid's Tale

Jane Austen
Mansfield Park

Jane Austen
Persuasion

Jane Austen
Pride and Prejudice

Alan Bennett
Talking Heads

William Blake
Songs of Innocence and of Experience

Charlotte Brontë
Jane Eyre

Emily Brontë
Wuthering Heights

Angela Carter
Nights at the Circus

Geoffrey Chaucer
The Franklin's Prologue and Tale

Geoffrey Chaucer
The Miller's Prologue and Tale

Geoffrey Chaucer
Prologue To the Canterbury Tales

Geoffrey Chaucer
The Wife of Bath's Prologue and Tale

Samuel Taylor Coleridge
Selected Poems

Joseph Conrad
Heart of Darkness

Daniel Defoe
Moll Flanders

Charles Dickens
Great Expectations

Charles Dickens
Hard Times

Emily Dickinson
Selected Poems

John Donne
Selected Poems

Carol Ann Duffy
Selected Poems

George Eliot
Middlemarch

George Eliot
The Mill on the Floss

T.S. Eliot
Selected Poems

F. Scott Fitzgerald
The Great Gatsby

E.M. Forster
A Passage to India

Brian Friel
Translations

Thomas Hardy
The Mayor of Casterbridge

Thomas Hardy
The Return of the Native

Thomas Hardy
Selected Poems

Thomas Hardy
Tess of the d'Urbervilles

Seamus Heaney
Selected Poems from Opened Ground

Nathaniel Hawthorne
The Scarlet Letter

Kazuo Ishiguro
The Remains of the Day

Ben Jonson
The Alchemist

James Joyce
Dubliners

John Keats
Selected Poems

Christopher Marlowe
Doctor Faustus

Arthur Miller
Death of a Salesman

John Milton
Paradise Lost Books I & II

Toni Morrison
Beloved

Sylvia Plath
Selected Poems

Alexander Pope
Rape of the Lock and other poems

William Shakespeare
Antony and Cleopatra

William Shakespeare
As You Like It

William Shakespeare
Hamlet

William Shakespeare
King Lear

William Shakespeare
Measure for Measure

William Shakespeare
The Merchant of Venice

William Shakespeare
A Midsummer Night's Dream

William Shakespeare
Much Ado About Nothing

William Shakespeare
Othello

William Shakespeare
Richard II

William Shakespeare
Romeo and Juliet

William Shakespeare
The Taming of the Shrew

William Shakespeare
The Tempest

William Shakespeare
Twelfth Night

William Shakespeare
The Winter's Tale

George Bernard Shaw
Saint Joan

Mary Shelley
Frankenstein

Jonathan Swift
Gulliver's Travels and A Modest Proposal

Alfred, Lord Tennyson
Selected Poems

Alice Walker
The Color Purple

Oscar Wilde
The Importance of Being Earnest

Tennessee Williams
A Streetcar Named Desire

John Webster
The Duchess of Malfi

Virginia Woolf
To the Lighthouse

W.B. Yeats
Selected Poems

Jane Austen
Emma

Jane Austen
Sense and Sensibility

Samuel Beckett
Waiting for Godot and
Endgame

Louis de Bernières
Captain Corelli's Mandolin

Charlotte Brontë
Villette

Caryl Churchill
Top Girls and *Cloud Nine*

Charles Dickens
Bleak House

T.S. Eliot
The Waste Land

Thomas Hardy
Jude the Obscure

Homer
The Iliad

Homer
The Odyssey

Aldous Huxley
Brave New World

D.H. Lawrence
Selected Poems

Christopher Marlowe
Edward II

George Orwell
Nineteen Eighty-four

Jean Rhys
Wide Sargasso Sea

William Shakespeare
Henry IV Pt I

William Shakespeare
Henry IV Part II

William Shakespeare
Macbeth

William Shakespeare ·
Richard III

Tom Stoppard
Arcadia and *Rosencrantz and
Guildenstern are Dead*

Virgil
The Aeneid

Jeanette Winterson
*Oranges are Not the Only
Fruit*

Tennessee Williams
Cat on a Hot Tin Roof

Metaphysical Poets

OTHER TITLES

GCSE and equivalent levels (£3.50 each)

Maya Angelou
I Know Why the Caged Bird Sings

Jane Austen
Pride and Prejudice

Alan Ayckbourn
Absent Friends

Elizabeth Barrett Browning
Selected Poems

Robert Bolt
A Man for All Seasons

Harold Brighouse
Hobson's Choice

Charlotte Brontë
Jane Eyre

Emily Brontë
Wuthering Heights

Shelagh Delaney
A Taste of Honey

Charles Dickens
David Copperfield

Charles Dickens
Great Expectations

Charles Dickens
Hard Times

Charles Dickens
Oliver Twist

Roddy Doyle
Paddy Clarke Ha Ha Ha

George Eliot
Silas Marner

George Eliot
The Mill on the Floss

Anne Frank
The Diary of Anne Frank

William Golding
Lord of the Flies

Oliver Goldsmith
She Stoops To Conquer

Willis Hall
The Long and the Short and the Tall

Thomas Hardy
Far from the Madding Crowd

Thomas Hardy
The Mayor of Casterbridge

Thomas Hardy
Tess of the d'Urbervilles

Thomas Hardy
The Withered Arm and other Wessex Tales

L.P. Hartley
The Go-Between

Seamus Heaney
Selected Poems

Susan Hill
I'm the King of the Castle

Barry Hines
A Kestrel for a Knave

Louise Lawrence
Children of the Dust

Harper Lee
To Kill a Mockingbird

Laurie Lee
Cider with Rosie

Arthur Miller
The Crucible

Arthur Miller
A View from the Bridge

Robert O'Brien
Z for Zachariah

Frank O'Connor
My Oedipus Complex and Other Stories

George Orwell
Animal Farm

J.B. Priestley
An Inspector Calls

J.B. Priestley
When We Are Married

Willy Russell
Educating Rita

Willy Russell
Our Day Out

J.D. Salinger
The Catcher in the Rye

William Shakespeare
Henry IV Part 1

William Shakespeare
Henry V

William Shakespeare
Julius Caesar

William Shakespeare
Macbeth

William Shakespeare
The Merchant of Venice

William Shakespeare
A Midsummer Night's Dream

William Shakespeare
Much Ado About Nothing

William Shakespeare
Romeo and Juliet

William Shakespeare
The Tempest

William Shakespeare
Twelfth Night

George Bernard Shaw
Pygmalion

Mary Shelley
Frankenstein

R.C. Sherriff
Journey's End

Rukshana Smith
Salt on the Snow

John Steinbeck
Of Mice and Men

Robert Louis Stevenson
Dr Jekyll and Mr Hyde

Jonathan Swift
Gulliver's Travels

Robert Swindells
Daz 4 Zoe

Mildred D. Taylor
Roll of Thunder, Hear My Cry

Mark Twain
Huckleberry Finn

James Watson
Talking in Whispers

Edith Wharton
Ethan Frome

William Wordsworth
Selected Poems

A Choice of Poets

Mystery Stories of the Nineteenth Century including The Signalman

Nineteenth Century Short Stories

Poetry of the First World War

Six Women Poets

Notes

NOTES